Christmas with Kim-Joy

A FESTIVE COLLECTION OF EDIBLE CUTENESS

Christmas with Kim-Joy

A FESTIVE COLLECTION OF EDIBLE CUTENESS

PHOTOGRAPHY BY ELLIS PARRINDER
ILLUSTRATIONS BY LINDA VAN DEN BERG
LETTERING DESIGN BY MARY KATE MᶜDEVITT

Hardie Grant

QUADRILLE

Contents

Introduction

Christmas and baking are inseparable! Every Christmas we think about all the baked treats and deliciousness that we are going to gobble up. So I wanted this book to include everyone's favourite Christmas baking and flavours, and then also some non-traditional recipes – because I love getting socks for Christmas, but then I also enjoy being surprised by something unexpected, like a ticket to go on a steam train! So this way, every recipe is like unwrapping a brand new present full of potential surprises, joy and tastiness.

Just like my last book, I've put tons of thought and effort into each and every bake to make sure it tastes amazing and comes to life right off the page! There are canelé trolls, marshmallow seals snoozing in igloos, Christmas mice living on stollen, snowmen choux gliding around, arctic foxes up to mischief, and so much more. It'll be hard not to start attaching personalities for each of your bakes! And of course, the book is full of colour and there are messages of positivity dotted about to keep you smiling and baking lots.

For those of you who are new to baking, there are some recipes I'd recommend over others. Where to start mostly depends on what area of baking you feel you're going to enjoy most! So that might be bread, cookie decorating, meringue, cakes or pastry. Have a look through and see what you feel is closest to being achievable (and most of all that you're likely to have fun making and eating!), then go from there, gradually building up your skills. There are step-by-step images for the recipes that benefit from them, and each bake can be decorated to the full, or kept simpler if you're not a decorator (or just want to eat that stollen warm from the oven!). Things are rarely perfect the first time, but eating the treats that don't quite turn out right is part of the fun in baking!

Also, I mentioned in my last book that mistakes sometimes become great design ideas, and that still applies in this book. You might make mistakes that don't go anywhere and you just have to eat them (oh, how terrible!), or you might make 'mistakes' that are the beginnings of brilliant new ideas. Be creative with your baking, and feel free to create your own versions of the bakes in this book. A lot of people see baking as being quite a rigid science with rules to follow, but I don't think it's as black and white as that. There's a lot of opportunity to create something unique.

I HOPE THAT YOU CAN FLICK THROUGH THIS BOOK AND HAVE A LITTLE ESCAPE FROM THE WORLD. AND THEN GO GET BAKING AND ENJOY IT!

Kim-Joy

> **The oven temperatures given are for fan-assisted [convection] ovens. If your oven is not fan-assisted, raise the temperature by 10–20˚C.**

Cookies

Shortbread

This recipe can be rolled out thinly and used to cut out your shapes, though you will need to take extra care as this dough has a high fat to flour ratio and is therefore a little more delicate. If you are new to working with cookie dough, then use this dough for more simple shapes rather than intricate ones.

You can flavour this however you like – some festive flavour suggestions are orange/lemon zest, ground nutmeg, ground cinnamon, ground ginger, ground cardamom, almond extract or mint extract (pairs well with dark chocolate).

MAKES: 24–30

200g [¾ cup plus 2 Tbsp] salted butter, at room temperature

85g [7 Tbsp] caster or granulated sugar

200g [1½ cups] plain [all-purpose] flour, plus extra for dusting

70g [¼ cup plus 1½ Tbsp] fine semolina

1 / Line a baking sheet that you can fit in the fridge with baking paper or a silicone mat. Beat the butter and sugar together in a large bowl until smooth and fluffy.

2 / Add the flour and semolina and mix until just combined. The dough should be slightly sticky, but soft and easy to handle. If necessary, wrap the dough in plastic wrap and chill for 10–15 minutes until firm enough to roll out.

3 / Turn out onto a well-floured work surface and roll out to about 3mm [⅛in] thick. Use cutters or templates to cut out desired shapes, and transfer to the prepared baking sheet.

4 / Refrigerate for 15 minutes, while you preheat the oven to 160°C [325°F/Gas mark 3].

5 / Bake for 10–15 minutes until just lightly browned at the edges. Leave to cool for 10 minutes on the baking sheet, then gently transfer to a wire rack to finish cooling. These can be left plain or decorated using royal icing (pages 15–17).

Basic Vegan Shortbread

This shortbread tastes like it is full of butter, thanks to the coconut oil, and people are always surprised that it's vegan. It has just a hint of sweetness, so it's perfect for covering with royal icing. If eating these plain, then sprinkle some caster or granulated sugar on top just before baking. You can also add 20–40g [1¼ Tbsp–3¼ Tbsp] more sugar to the dough, but this will make the shortbread a little more chewy rather than crumbly.

MAKES: 24–30

225g [1¾ cups] plain [all-purpose] flour, plus extra for dusting
130g [⅔ cup] organic extra virgin coconut oil (solid and scoopable)

40g [3¼ Tbsp] caster or granulated sugar
30–50ml [2–3½ Tbsp] cold water

1 / Line a baking sheet that will fit in your fridge with baking paper or a silicone mat. Add the flour to a large bowl, then add the scoopable coconut oil and rub it into the flour using your fingers. Stir in the sugar, then add just enough cold water to bring the dough together into a ball.

2 / Turn the dough out onto a lightly floured work surface and roll out until it is 3–5mm [⅛–¼in] thick.

Use cutters or templates to cut out your desired shapes. Transfer the shapes to the prepared baking sheet and chill for 15 minutes while you preheat the oven to 160°C [325°F/Gas mark 3].

3 / Bake for 10–15 minutes until just starting to colour at the edges. Leave to cool on the baking sheet for 5 minutes, before transferring to a wire rack to finish cooling.

Speculoos

In Belgium, speculoos are traditionally eaten in the run-up to St Nicholas Day (6 December), but you will find yourself enjoying them all year round, as they are beautifully spiced and delicious dunked in a cup of tea or just on their own. This recipe specifies cassonade sugar (which is tricky to find but you can buy it online in speciality Belgian shops), which will give it that caramel flavour you are looking for in a good speculoos. You can substitute this with light brown muscovado sugar and it will still taste amazing, but just not caramelized as much.

MAKES: 30–40

250g [1 cup plus 2 Tbsp] salted butter (or replace with vegan butter – for the best results, use vegan butter that's close to 80% fat)
250g [1¼ cups] brown cassonade sugar (or light brown muscovado sugar)

¾ tsp ground cinnamon
¼ tsp ground nutmeg
⅛ tsp ground white pepper
⅛ tsp ground cloves
⅛ tsp ground cardamom
pinch of ground anise

¼ tsp bicarbonate of soda [baking soda]
½ egg (or 2 Tbsp aquafaba [chickpea water])
350g [2⅔ cups] plain [all-purpose] flour (or gluten-free flour plus ⅓ tsp xanthan gum)

1 / Line a baking sheet with baking paper or a silicone mat and set aside for now. Cream the butter and cassonade sugar in a stand mixer fitted with a balloon whisk attachment until the butter and sugar is soft, fluffy and paler in colour. Scrape the sides and base of the bowl occasionally.

2 / Add all the spices, bicarbonate of soda and egg or aquafaba, then mix for a few more seconds until completely combined.

3 / Remove the bowl from the stand mixer and add all the flour. Use your hands to rub the butter and sugar mixture into the flour, then combine into a ball.

4 / Roll out the dough to just under 3mm [⅛in] thick, then use cutters to cut into desired shapes. Transfer to the lined baking sheet and chill in the fridge for at least 20 minutes.

5 / When you are ready to bake, preheat the oven to 180°C [350°F/Gas mark 4].

6 / Bake for about 15 minutes, or until the edges are just starting to colour. Transfer to a wire rack and leave to cool.

Ginger Cookies

This cookie dough is a good alternative to the speculoos when you're making gingerbread houses.

MAKES: 30–40

150g [⅔ cup] salted butter
120g [½ cup plus 1½ Tbsp]
   dark muscovado [soft
   brown] sugar

2 tsp black treacle
   [molasses]
2 Tbsp beaten egg
2 Tbsp ground ginger

¾ Tbsp ground cinnamon
¼ tsp ground cloves
225g [1⅔ cups] plain
   [all-purpose] flour

1 / Line a baking sheet with baking paper. Place the butter, sugar and treacle in a stand mixer (or use a handheld electric whisk) fitted with the balloon whisk attachment and mix on high speed until fluffy. Add the beaten egg and spices and mix briefly.

2 / Add the flour and combine into a ball with your hands. Turn out onto a floured surface and roll out to the thickness of a coin. Use cutters or templates to cut out your desired shapes, then transfer to the prepared baking sheet and refrigerate for 15 minutes. Preheat the oven to 170°C [340°F/Gas mark 3].

3 / Bake for 10–12 minutes until just beginning to colour. Leave to cool for 10 minutes on the sheet, then gently transfer to a rack to finish cooling.

Cookie Decorating Tips & Ideas

ROYAL ICING CONSISTENCY

Different people like to work with different consistencies, but I like to work with what is called a '15-second icing'. This means that after stirring the mixture, the surface will return back to its former smooth state in about 15 seconds. This consistency will work for both outlining AND flooding, so is much easier than making two batches. The definition of '15-second icing' varies for everyone though, as everyone counts differently, so it's mostly about practising and getting the feel for the correct consistency. My royal icing recipe on the following page should get you to roughly the consistency you will need, so hopefully you can work from there!

If icing can get back to being smooth in 15 seconds, maybe you can too! Take your time with this.

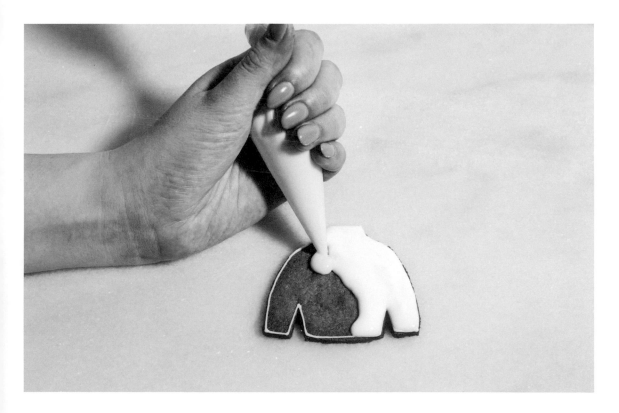

ROYAL ICING RECIPE
This makes enough for a decent number of cookies

40g [1½oz] egg white (substitute with aquafaba for a vegan version)

225g [1⅔ cups] icing [confectioners'] sugar

plus extra egg white (or aquafaba) and icing [confectioners'] sugar to adjust and get the right consistency

Use a stand mixer (or handheld electric whisk) fitted with a balloon whisk attachment to combine the egg white/aquafaba and icing sugar until you get a smooth consistency. Then add tiny amounts of extra egg white (or aquafaba) and/or icing sugar to get the right consistency. Add food dye to colour as desired! That's it!

DISPOSABLE PIPING BAGS
Good disposable piping [pastry] bags are your friends! You want to buy some that don't have a seam, as this can get in the way when piping. For outlining and for piping intricate details, cut a teeny tiny tip from your piping bag. For flooding, cut a slightly bigger tip (depends on how big an area you are flooding). That's it. No need for piping nozzles, which make washing up a lot harder! If you ever cut a tip that's too big, or want to change to a smaller opening, then just pop the piping bag into another piping bag. Cut the tip as desired and continue!

COOKIE PREP, PLANNING AND LAYERING
It helps to draw a guide of where you will pipe the outlines, directly on the cookie. It also helps to know what colours you are going to use before you start, so you can mix them all up and put into piping bags. I don't always know what colours I will want, so I always leave some white royal icing in a bowl that I can dye later. Just make sure to cover the bowl with plastic wrap, as the surface will crust up quickly.

Sometimes things come to you as you go along. A vague idea is all you need. That's okay too.

Cookie decorating does take some forward planning if you want to do more than one layer, in which case you would wait a few hours for the first layer to dry before working on the second, or third. For instance, you may have a background layer using the wet-on-wet technique to create a sunset, and then after that dries you might want to pipe some mountains on top of that, then add some painted birds. Or you might want to pipe some tiny flower detailing on a dress. The layer underneath would need to be dry before you can do all these things. While your biscuits are drying, set them aside and find something to do (or not do!) to relax.

OUTLINING
When you first start piping royal icing in a neat line, you might find it tricky. It's not like dragging a pen across a surface. You need to pipe, lift and ease the line where you need it. *Don't expect to be perfect the first time! Practise and you will get better.*

FLOODING
No, not the psychological therapy used to overcome phobias – this is much nicer.

Once you've planned and then outlined your cookie, it's time to flood. All you are doing is just filling the space inside, and the outline will stop it leaking over. Use a cocktail stick [toothpick] to even it out and get rid of any bubbles before it sets.

WET ON WET
This is when you use two different colours and a toothpick to create some interesting effects. This is useful for polka dots, hearts, flowers and scenes that involve a beautiful gradient of colour (e.g. sunsets, skies, seas, fire).

PAINTING ON ROYAL ICING
When your royal icing is completely dry (4–6 hours, but I generally just wait overnight to be sure), you can paint on it using food dyes or lustre dusts mixed with vodka (it evaporates quicker than water). You can also brush on lustre dusts to give depth, and draw on the icing using edible ink pens – anything you can paint or draw, you can do on an iced cookie.

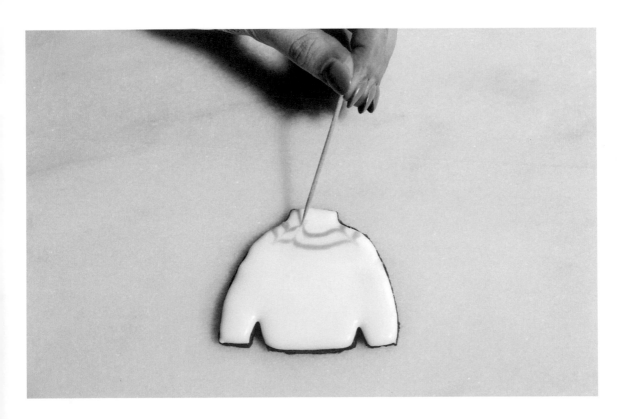

Cakes

Matcha Bamboo Swiss Roll with Festive Pandas

Swiss roll [jelly roll] can be daunting when it comes to the critical moment to roll up, as there is always the fear that cracks will appear, but as long as you carefully follow the steps and roll the cake while it's still warm (and don't forget to trim the drier edges off first!), you can't go far wrong. The pandas are optional of course, but really bring the bamboo cake roll into context. As a bonus, they can be used to disguise any cracks – so all of the pandas, but none of the pandemonium!

SERVES: 8

CAKE
butter, for greasing
4 medium eggs
125g [⅔ cup minus 2 tsp] caster or granulated sugar
125g [1 cup minus 1 Tbsp] self-raising flour (to make gluten free, substitute with gluten-free flour, ½ tsp xanthan gum and ¾ tsp baking powder)
2 tsp matcha powder

FILLING
3–4 Tbsp strawberry jam
180ml [¾ cup] double [heavy] cream

30g [3½ Tbsp] icing [confectioners'] sugar
1 tsp vanilla bean paste

PLUS (TO DECORATE)
green ribbon
1 quantity Royal Icing (page 16)
black food dye

about 10 white marshmallows
festive sprinkles, candy canes and fondant

"You may feel like everything's gone wrong, but it's not all black and white. There's often a pawsibility things will get better!"

1 / Grease a rectangular 38 x 25-cm [15 x 10-in] Swiss [jelly] roll tin with butter, then line the base with baking paper. It helps if you have some baking paper hanging over 2 sides, so you can lift out the roll easily. Preheat the oven to 180°C [350°F/Gas mark 4].

2 / Whisk the eggs and caster sugar together in a stand mixer fitted with a balloon whisk attachment on high speed for 7 minutes. You can use a handheld electric whisk, but it will take longer. Sift in the flour (or gluten-free flour mixture) and matcha, then carefully fold in to avoid deflating the batter too much.

3 / Spoon the batter into the prepared baking tin and smooth with the back of a spatula. Bake for 10 minutes, or until spongy on top.

4 / Once baked, use a knife to loosen the sides, then use the paper to lift the cake out of the tin onto a chopping board. Trim all the edges, then lift and place on a wire rack, and immediately roll up along with the paper. Leave the cake to cool completely.

5 / When the cake is cool, carefully unroll it and spread over the jam. Whip the double cream with the icing sugar and vanilla bean paste to soft peaks. Spread the cream on top, then re-roll the cake up, peeling off the paper as you go along.

6 / Place the roll on a serving plate and use green ribbon to loop around the cake at 2 points, tying at the bottom to shape the cake so that it looks more like bamboo.

7 / Make the royal icing (page 16) and stir in enough black food dye to achieve the desired colour. Pipe this onto marshmallows to create pandas. You can cut some marshmallows smaller and arrange them differently to create different types of panda. Use festive sprinkles, candy canes and fondant to decorate the pandas further and create a Christmas panda scene.

Lemon & Cinnamon Swirl Bundt Cake

The key to a light cake is to cream the butter and sugar together until it's almost white in colour and very fluffy. You can't overwhisk, so keep going until it's taken to its limit. A stand mixer really helps, though you can use a handheld electric whisk (although you may get bored of waiting!). As a bonus, the icing decoration on this bundt is easy to achieve and the snowmen are fun to create. If you're feeling confident with sugarwork, then try the sugar 'glass' dome too, as this transforms the cake into something extra magical.

SERVES: 8

CAKE
300g [1½ cups] caster or
  granulated sugar
250g [1 cup plus 2 Tbsp]
  unsalted butter,
  softened, plus extra
  for greasing
1 tsp salt
6 medium eggs (250g
  [9oz])
350g [2⅔ cups] plain [all-
  purpose] flour (to make
  gluten free, substitute
  with gluten-free flour plus
  1 tsp xanthan gum)

grated zest of 3 lemons
1½ tsp baking powder
  (make sure you are
  using gluten-free baking
  powder if making this
  gluten free)
200g [¾ cup plus 2 Tbsp]
  sour cream

CINNAMON SWIRL
50g [¼ cup] light brown
  muscovado sugar
1 Tbsp ground cinnamon
1 tsp ground ginger
¼ tsp ground nutmeg

ROSEMARY TREES
rosemary sprigs
1 egg white
granulated sugar

SUGAR GLASS BALLOON
1 balloon
150g [¾ cup] caster or
  granulated sugar
100g [⅓ cup plus 1 Tbsp]
  liquid glucose
35ml [2 Tbsp] water

LEMON DRIZZLE
225g [1⅔ cups] icing
  [confectioners'] sugar
2–4 Tbsp lemon juice
white food dye

PLUS
white marshmallows
sprinkles of your choice
edible black ink pen
orange fondant or orange
  candy melts
hard pretzels, matchsticks,
  pocky or similar

1 / Preheat the oven to 160°C [325°F/Gas mark 3] and generously grease a 2.4-litre [80-fl oz] bundt tin with butter.

2 / Cream the sugar, butter and salt together in a stand mixer fitted with a balloon whisk attachment on high speed until fluffy and light in colour. You can use a handheld electric whisk but it will take longer.

3 / Add the eggs, one at a time, whisking for a good minute or so after each addition.

4 / Add the flour (or gluten-free flour plus xanthan gum), lemon zest and baking powder and whisk until just combined. Don't overwhisk.

5 / Add the sour cream and stir until just combined (again avoid overwhisking).

6 / Transfer 300g [10½oz] of the cake batter to a separate bowl, then add all the ingredients for the cinnamon swirl to this bowl and stir until just combined.

"Kindness snowballs."

7 / Layer the cake batter in the prepared bundt tin, alternating between spoonfuls of lemon batter and cinnamon swirl. Once all the batter is in the tin, use a chopstick (or similar) to swirl the batter a little.

8 / Bake for 50–60 minutes until a skewer inserted into the cake comes out clean.

9 / While the cake is baking, prepare the rosemary trees. Dip the rosemary sprigs in the egg white, then roll in the granulated sugar until coated. Leave to dry on baking paper.

10 / Next, make the sugar glass balloon. Fill a balloon with cold water from the tap, then knot the top. Place the balloon, knot side down, in a bowl (smaller than the balloon so that sugar doesn't drip and attach to the bowl). Make sure to have some baking paper underneath the bowl to stop sugar sticking to your work surface.

11 / Add the caster sugar, liquid glucose and water to a small pan and stir to combine. Heat over a high heat, but don't stir at all until the mixture reaches 150°C [300°F]. At this point, remove the pan from the heat and leave to cool to 130–133°C [226–271°F] (it will cool quite quickly so keep an eye on it). Immediately pour over the balloon in a circular

motion, then leave for about 10–15 minutes until set. Lift the balloon off the bowl and hold over the sink. Use scissors to cut a small hole at the base, letting the water drain out (try to avoid the water touching the sugar). You will then be able to gently pull the balloon away from the sugar glass. Set aside for now on some baking paper.

12 / When the bundt cake has finished baking, leave it to cool in its tin for 10 minutes, then turn out onto a wire rack. It should slide out easily; though if not give it a couple of firm taps.

13 / When the bundt is completely cool, make the lemon drizzle by whisking the icing sugar and lemon juice together in a bowl. Add a little white food dye. This will make the icing [frosting] bright white and opaque, which will look much more effective on the cake.

14 / Spoon the icing over the bundt cake, creating drips like the top of a mountain, then top with the sugar glass bowl and place the rosemary trees behind it. Arrange white marshmallows in the icing to look like snowmen. Use sprinkles, edible ink pen, orange fondant/candy melts and cookies (matchsticks or pocky work well) to decorate the snowmen. leave to cool.

Gingerbread Houses

You can't have Christmas without gingerbread houses! You can make these using any of the base cookie recipes on pages 10–13 (the speculoos base was used for the houses pictured on pages 33 and 35), OR you can get creative with storebought cookies. I've included ideas and inspiration for both options on the following pages.

If you use storebought cookies, the great thing is that you can play about with the construction as you go along. This is a good option if you don't trust your architectural planning skills! And you can get really creative with it.

Most importantly, just have fun with it and experiment with cookies, piping, candy, sprinkles, chocolate, everything! And then create your own creatures who live in the houses. There are endless possibilities…

YOU WILL NEED
Base recipe (see pages 10–13 – speculoos and gingerbread are the sturdiest),
   and/or storebought cookies
Royal Icing (see page 16)
Any candy, chocolates, sprinkles, and general edible decorations you like!

> Tip: If you're working with larger cookie dough panels, roll the dough out directly on the baking paper and cut to size directly on there. Then just remove the excess dough around the cut-outs. If you were to lift the panels up to transfer them, it would likely result in the shape distorting, though small panels are usually fine. Also, if your panels distort after baking, trim the edges with a sharp knife while they are still warm.

When you make your own cookie panels for your gingerbread houses, you need to have a general plan, as you will need to make templates from card. But it's a lot easier than it looks – you need 2 identical panels for the front and back, 2 identical panels for the side walls, and lastly 2 identical panels for the roof. So 3 unique panels in all.

When you have baked the individual pieces of your house, leave the pieces to cool completely before starting construction. Build the base before adding the roof panels one at a time.

You will need a sturdy royal icing (see advice and recipe on pages 15–16). Royal icing is easy to use and can be wiped off if it goes wrong. For small- to medium-sized houses, it's the perfect 'glue'! Just make sure to hold the roof on for a little while – the steeper and/or heavier the roof, the longer you need to hold it. The nice thing is that you can also use the same icing to pipe all the small details on. But if you're creating large houses, a hard crack caramel is best, though it is harder to work with!

You can also combine homemade cookie panels with storebought extras: for example, make your own pieces for the house, then add ready-made cookies or candy to create the rooftop.

Macarons Tips

I use the Italian meringue method for making macarons as I find it is less temperamental and doesn't take much longer to prepare. Ideally, you need a stand mixer for these as it involves multitasking and then whisking egg white at high speed – while pouring hot sugar onto them. You will also need a sugar thermometer for the sugar syrup. But these things are worth it for a beautiful macaron!

Macarons are tricky, so don't be disheartened if they don't work out the first time. Expect to try these a few times before you get them right! Here are some helpful tips:

• Make sure your almonds are ground up very finely. I find that storebought ground almonds in the UK are not fine enough, so I process them in a spice grinder just for a few seconds (not TOO long otherwise they release their oils and turn into nut butter), then sift the ground almonds to remove any larger pieces.

• It helps to have an oven thermometer, and not to have oven hotspots for an even bake! An oven thermometer helps, as sometimes your oven is not the temperature you think it is, and macarons are so sensitive to oven temperature.

• I recommend a flat surface and a macaron template. I used to pipe my macarons on baking paper, which does work, but you just need to make sure it is very flat and preferably without any creases. If it isn't, then some of your macarons might become misshapen. I now prefer to use a non-stick silicone baking mat as this won't crease. You can place any template or guides underneath the silicone mat as they are slightly see-through. You can also buy silicone mats with circle markings to guide you when piping.

• When piping, pipe from straight above rather than at an angle. This helps to achieve a round and even shape.

• Don't skip banging the baking sheet on the work surface – this is important to get any large air bubbles out. If you don't, they may expand and cause the macaron surface to crack!

• Give the macarons time to rest and form a skin! You can chill out and enjoy a break while they do. Again, this helps them to form feet and not crack on the surface.

• These Italian meringue macarons don't need folding for as long as French macarons do. Once you can lift the spatula and the batter falls down like a ribbon and can form a figure-of-eight on the rest of the batter in the bowl, don't fold any more. It is always better to underfold than overfold. Remember that as you transfer the batter to the piping [pastry] bag, you are essentially folding it further.

Macarons

MAKES: 1½ BAKING SHEETS OF MACARONS

115g [½ cup plus 1 Tbsp] caster
  or granulated sugar
40ml [2⅔ Tbsp] water

MIXTURE A

105g [1 cup] finely ground and
  sifted almonds
105g [¾ cup plus 2 Tbsp] sifted
  icing [confectioners'] sugar
40g [1½oz] egg white
  (or aquafaba)

MIXTURE B

45g [1½oz] egg whites,
  at room temperature
  (or aquafaba)

TO MAKE VEGAN MACARONS

It's easy to make vegan macarons: follow the main recipe opposite but just switch the egg white for aquafaba (chickpea water) – and it's best if you can reduce down the aquafaba beforehand, so that its consistency is similar to egg whites (see below). You also need to bake the vegan version at a lower temperature for longer, as they are more sensitive to heat, but other than that, the same rules apply for both!

To reduce down aquafaba, you will need 85g [⅓ cup] aquafaba in total. So start with 170g [¾ cup] aquafaba (the liquid drained from a can of chickpeas [garbanzo beans]) and pour this into a pan. Simmer over a medium heat until you have 85–90g [⅓ cup] aquafaba remaining. You will need to estimate when it's reduced by about half and then weigh it. If it isn't quite there, give it a little more time and then re-weigh. Leave the aquafaba to cool to room temperature before using it in the recipe. This stuff doesn't look particularly appetizing but have faith – it does work!

- MACARONS & MERINGUES -

1 / First, line 2 baking sheets with baking paper or silicone mats. Have any templates ready to hand and organized. Have all your piping [pastry] bags and any food dyes you will be using ready to hand.

2 / For Mixture A, stir the sifted ground almonds and icing sugar together in a large bowl. Add the egg white (or aquafaba) and mix together until it forms a paste.

3 / Add Mixture B to a stand mixer fitted with a balloon whisk attachment.

4 / Add the caster sugar and water to a pan and stir occasionally over a medium-high heat until the sugar has dissolved and the mixture starts to bubble. Start whisking the egg white (or aquafaba) in the stand mixer to soft peaks. You want to time the sugar syrup to reach 115°C [239°F] with the egg white (or aquafaba) reaching soft peaks. You can always take the sugar syrup off the heat and/or slow the mixer (but don't turn it off) to time the two together.

The aquafaba will take longer to whisk to soft peaks than the egg whites, so bear this in mind when timing this with the sugar syrup reaching 115°C [239°F].

5 / When the egg white (or aquafaba) has reached soft peaks and the sugar syrup is at 115°C [239°F], increase the speed of the mixer to high while pouring the sugar syrup in a thin steady stream down the side of the bowl (being careful not to pour the syrup directly on the whisk).

6 / Once all the sugar syrup has been poured in, continue whisking on high speed until the side of the bowl feels cool to the touch, 3–5 minutes or so. At this point, turn off the mixer and use a spatula to fold the meringue into Mixture A. Add food dye to colour. If using multiple colours, distribute the macaron batter between bowls and colour each individually before transferring to piping bags.

- MACARONS & MERINGUES -

7 / Pipe the macarons onto the prepared baking sheets or mats (and following templates if using). If the macaron batter is the correct consistency, the macarons should spread slightly after piping but still hold their shape, and the tip of the macarons should disappear within a minute or so.

8 / After piping, pick up the sheet and bang it on a flat surface about 3 times. You should see air bubbles come to the surface. Some of them might pop of their own accord, but you might have to use a cocktail stick [toothpick] to help pop a few *(which is very satisfying!)*

9 / Leave the macarons for at least 1–2 hours to form a skin on the surface – you should be able to gently touch the macaron and it shouldn't come away on your finger. The time it takes for the macarons to form a skin depends on how humid the air is, so it could take longer.

10 / When the macarons are ready, preheat the oven to 150°C [300°F/Gas mark 2] (or 120°C [248°F/ Gas mark ½] for vegan macarons). Bake the egg white-based macarons for about 15 minutes and the vegan macarons for 30 minutes.

11 / Leave the macarons to cool before peeling them off the baking paper and then filling (and decorating) with the options on the following pages. The macarons are best chilled in the fridge for a day or so before serving, as this helps to soften the shell – this is especially the case for vegan macarons as they tend to be crunchier due to their longer baking time.

White Ganache for Macarons

These are some basic macaron filling recipes so that you can mix and match! You can also experiment with other fruit curds, and there are endless options for flavouring the ganache. The vegan white chocolate ganache alternative is a delicious and creamy option if you don't have vegan white chocolate to hand.

There are so many ways to flavour this. Some festive suggestions are: orange zest, ground cinnamon, ground ginger, orange blossom or ground cardamom. Add ganache flavours to the chocolate while whisking but before it has thickened, or infuse into the heated cream/coconut milk (this is better for things like cardamom and orange zest). You can also pipe a ring around the macaron, then add a different flavour to the centre. Some ideas are: small pieces of crystallized [candied] ginger in the centre, curds, caramel, jam, etc.

MAKES: ENOUGH TO FILL 14–16 MACARONS

WHITE CHOCOLATE GANACHE
110g [4oz] white chocolate
70ml [⅓ cup] double [heavy] cream

VEGAN WHITE CHOCOLATE GANACHE
110g [4oz] vegan white chocolate
70ml [⅓ cup] coconut milk

VEGAN WHITE CHOCOLATE GANACHE ALTERNATIVE
50g [1¾oz] cocoa butter
25g [1oz] coconut oil
65g [¼ cup plus 2 Tbsp] icing [confectioners'] sugar
50ml [3⅓ Tbsp] coconut milk

1 / To make either of the first two ganaches, chop the chocolate into small, roughly even-sized pieces. Add the chocolate to a heatproof bowl.

2 / Add the double cream or coconut milk to a saucepan and bring to a simmer over a medium/ high heat. When it is starting to bubble, pour it on top of the chocolate. Make sure the cream covers all of the chocolate pieces. Leave to stand for 3 minutes, then stir to combine all the cream and chocolate. The chocolate should be completely melted by now. If not, pour it back into a pan and gently heat until the chocolate has melted.

3 / Add the mixture to a bowl, cover with plastic wrap and set aside until cooled to room temperature, then whisk until lightened in colour and the right thickness for filling macarons. While whisking, add your desired flavourings (e.g. flavouring oils, pistachio paste, etc.). The ganache will take a little while to thicken, but it will reach a point and suddenly start to thicken quite quickly, so avoid overwhipping as it will become too difficult to pipe. Transfer to a piping [pastry] bag and use to fill macarons.

VEGAN ALTERNATIVE

1 / Add the cocoa butter and coconut oil to a saucepan and melt over a low heat.

2 / Pour into a bowl, add the icing sugar and whisk together until smooth. Add the coconut milk and continue whisking until the mixture becomes whiter in colour, fluffy and a pipeable consistency. While whisking, you can add your desired flavourings. The mixture will take a while to thicken so be patient with it, and it helps to use a stand mixer as you will need to whisk it for at least 5 minutes. Transfer to a piping bag and use to fill your macarons.

Dark Ganache for Macarons

You can also add a little liqueur (e.g. amaretto), almond extract, other flavouring oils (e.g. mint), ground cardamom or orange zest to your ganache for flavour. Alternatively, make a praline paste and mix in to add another dimension. Also try adding a little salt. Add these to the chocolate when melted but before it has set, or infuse into the heated cream/coconut milk (this is better for things like cardamom and orange zest). Again, you can also pipe a ring of ganache and add different flavours to the centre. Try crystallized [candied] ginger, caramel or peanut.

MAKES: ENOUGH TO FILL 14–16 MACARONS

DARK CHOCOLATE GANACHE
80g [3oz] dark [bittersweet] chocolate
80ml [⅓ cup] double [heavy] cream
20g [2¼ Tbsp] icing [confectioners'] sugar, or to taste (this depends on the sweetness of your dark chocolate)

VEGAN DARK CHOCOLATE GANACHE
80g [3oz] vegan dark chocolate
80ml [⅓ cup] coconut milk
20g [2¼ Tbsp] icing [confectioners'] sugar, or to taste (this depends on the sweetness of your dark chocolate)

1 / Chop the chocolate into small, roughly equal pieces. Add the chocolate to a heatproof bowl.

2 / Add the double cream or coconut milk to a saucepan and bring to a simmer over a medium/high heat. When it is starting to bubble, pour it on top of the chocolate. Make sure the cream covers all of the chocolate pieces. Leave to stand for 3 minutes, then stir to combine all the cream and chocolate. The chocolate should be completely melted by now. If not, pour it back into a pan and gently heat until the chocolate has melted. Stir in the sugar, if using.

3 / Add the mixture to a bowl, cover with plastic wrap and set aside until cooled to room temperature, then whisk until lightened in colour and the right thickness for filling macarons. While whisking, add your desired flavourings (e.g. flavouring oils, pistachio paste, etc.). The ganache will take a little while to thicken, but it will reach a point and suddenly start to thicken quite quickly, so avoid overwhipping as it will become too difficult to pipe. Transfer to a piping [pastry] bag and use to fill macarons.

- MACARONS & MERINGUES -

Orange Curd for Macarons

MAKES: ENOUGH TO FILL 14–16 MACARONS

2 egg yolks
grated zest and juice of
    1 large orange (about
    100ml [7 Tbsp])

100g [½ cup] caster or
    granulated sugar
60g [¼ cup] unsalted
    butter

1 / Add the egg yolks, orange zest and juice, sugar and butter to a heatproof bowl and stir with a balloon whisk until combined.

2 / Place the bowl over a saucepan of gently simmering water, making sure the base of the bowl doesn't touch the water, and whisk constantly for 10–15 minutes until the mixture has thickened (you will notice the foam start to disappear) and holds a trail.

3 / Pour the curd into a bowl, cover with plastic wrap (touching the surface to avoid it forming a skin) and place in the fridge before using to fill macarons. You can strain the curd before transferring to a bowl if you have any bits of cooked egg, or if you prefer not to have the zest.

Vegan Alternative

grated zest and juice of
    1 large orange (about
    100ml [7 Tbsp])
100g [½ cup] caster or
    granulated sugar

1¼ Tbsp arrowroot powder
    or cornflour [cornstarch]
40g [¼ cup] coconut oil
30ml [2 Tbsp] coconut milk

1 / Combine the orange zest, juice, sugar and arrowroot or cornflour in a small saucepan and stir constantly over a medium heat until the mixture is thickened and coats the back of a spoon.

2 / Take off the heat, then immediately add the coconut oil and coconut milk and stir until completely melted and combined.

3 / Pour the mixture into a bowl and cover with plastic wrap (making sure it touches the surface of the curd to avoid it forming a film). Freeze for 1 hour. It won't seem very thick right now, but will thicken to the perfect consistency as it cools.

Meringues

The method for both vegan and non-vegan meringues is essentially the same – the only difference is that the vegan meringues take a little longer to whisk to soft peaks initially, and the vegan meringues are best baked until completely dry in the centre. Remember the purpose of putting meringues in the oven is to dry them out rather than cook them, so don't be tempted to turn the oven up higher!

MAKES: 1 LARGE BAKING SHEET OF MERINGUES

MERINGUE	VEGAN MERINGUE
120g [⅔ cup] caster or granulated sugar	120g [⅔ cup] caster or granulated sugar
80g [2¾oz] egg white	80g [⅓ cup] aquafaba
pinch of cream of tartar (optional)	pinch of cream of tartar (optional)

1 / Preheat the oven to 200°C [400°F/Gas mark 6]. Line a baking sheet with baking paper and spread out the caster sugar on the sheet. Place in the oven for 7–8 minutes until the sugar is warm but not caramelized, discarding any bits that are caramelized and replacing with an equal weight of caster sugar. Leave the oven door open to allow it to cool down to 100°C [210°F/Gas mark ¼].

2 / Add the egg white (or aquafaba) to a stand mixer fitted with a balloon whisk attachment (you can use a handheld electric whisk but you will be whisking for a long time, so a stand mixer is ideal). Mix on high speed until you have soft peaks, then gradually add the sugar, 1 Tbsp at a time, whisking for about 30 seconds–1 minute after each addition.

It is important to add the sugar very slowly so that it all dissolves properly.

3 / When all the sugar has been incorporated (the meringue should feel smooth and not gritty between your fingers), add the cream of tartar, if using, then use a spatula to transfer the meringue to a piping [pastry] bag.

4 / Pipe desired meringue shapes onto a baking sheet lined with baking paper or a silicone mat and bake for 45–60 minutes for meringues that are gooey in the centre, or bake for 1 hour 30 minutes, then switch off the oven and leave the oven door closed for a few hours to completely crisp and dry the meringues.

MERINGUE CHRISTMAS WREATHS
Use an open-star nozzle to pipe a green meringue in a circle. Top with sprinkles and pipe a bow using red meringue (cut a small tip on the piping [pastry] bag), then bake.

MERINGUES WITH COLOUR
You can add gel food dye to the meringue mixture before baking, or you can paint thin stripes of gel food dye in the piping [pastry] bag, before filling with meringue and then piping. Experiment with different colours and effects.

MERINGUE SNOWMEN
Pipe a meringue blob, then pipe a smaller meringue blob on top. Dip your finger in water and use this to smooth down the tip of the meringue. Bake as normal, then decorate with Royal Icing (page 16).

MERINGUE CHRISTMAS TREES
Use a large open-star nozzle to pipe meringues in a swirl, starting wider at the base and finishing with a small tip. Top with sprinkles before baking. You can use different coloured meringue and sprinkles. After baking, add further details, such as edible silver dust.

MERINGUE POLAR BEARS
Pipe a meringue blob, then pipe a smaller meringue blob on top. Dip your finger in water and use this to smooth down the tip of the meringue. Using white meringue in a piping [pastry] bag with a smaller opening, pipe the polar bear ears, arms and legs, then bake. After baking, use coloured Royal Icing (page 16) to pipe the nose and hat. Use edible ink pen (or coloured royal icing again) for the eyes and detailing on the nose.

Breads

Penguin Mincemeat Bao

It's penguining to look a lot like Christmas... and you will love this soft and fluffy bread contrasted with the sweet and sticky vegetarian mincemeat (minced dried fruit) – a little twist on the traditional British mince pie.

Tip: To reheat these, just steam again before serving.

MAKES: 10–12

MINCEMEAT (OPTIONAL)

125g [½ cup plus 1 Tbsp] salted butter
200g [1½ cups] currants
200g [1 generous cup] sultanas [golden raisins]
200g [1¼ cups] raisins
200g [1⅔ cups] dried cranberries
50g [⅓ cup] glacé [candied] cherries, finely chopped
60g [½ cup] pecans, finely chopped
3 cooking [baking] apples, peeled and finely chopped
250g [1¼ cups] light muscovado sugar
grated zest and juice of 2 oranges
grated zest of 2 lemons and juice of 1 lemon
4 tsp mixed spice
1 tsp ground cinnamon
1¼ tsp ground nutmeg
150ml [⅔ cup] brandy (or fruit juice)

BAO DOUGH

300g [2¼ cups] plain [all-purpose] flour, plus extra for dusting
3g [½ tsp] fast-action dried [active dry] yeast
3g [½ tsp] salt
60g [5 Tbsp] caster or granulated sugar
90ml [⅓ cup plus 1 Tbsp] whole milk (will also work with plant-based milk to make vegan)
85ml [⅓ cup] water
1 Tbsp vegetable oil, plus extra for oiling

PLUS

orange and black gel food dyes
mincemeat

1 / For the mincemeat, if making, melt the butter in a large pan over a low heat, then add all the ingredients, except the brandy. Bring the heat up to a slow simmer and cook for about 10 minutes, or until the apples are soft. Stir occasionally so the ingredients at the base of the pan don't burn. Leave to cool completely, then add the brandy. Stir, then transfer to sterilized jars.

2 / For the bao, add the flour, yeast, salt and sugar to a stand mixer fitted with a dough hook attachment.

3 / Add the milk, water and vegetable oil and let the machine knead the mixture for about 8 minutes, or until the dough is smooth and elastic.

4 / Turn the dough out onto a very lightly floured work surface. Tear off a small piece (about 15g [½oz]) and knead in orange gel food dye until the colour is well distributed. Tear off a larger piece (about 110g [4oz]) and knead in some black gel food dye until the colour is well distributed.

5 / Place the dough in 3 separate oiled bowls and cover with plastic wrap. Leave in a warm place for about 1 hour, or until the dough has increased about 50 per cent in size.

"The more pract-ice you get, the better a baker you will become."

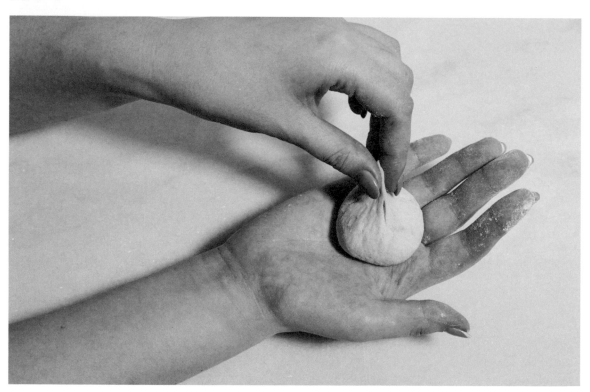

6 / Divide the plain dough into 12 x 38g [1¼oz] pieces. They will be a bit sticky, so be sure to coat your hands and the dough with flour when handling. To shape the bao, use your fingers to stretch the dough into a small circle, which is thinner at the edges than in the centre, then spoon 1 heaped tsp of mincemeat into the centre.

7 / Gather the edges up and press together to seal in the filling. Turn the bun smooth side up. Try to make sure the surface is as smooth as possible, and it helps to rotate the bao while pressing the palms of your hands together to ensure it's nice and tall to start with (it will naturally spread sideways when steamed).

8 / Next, roll out a small piece of the black dough, then stamp out a circle using a 3–3.5-cm [1¼-in] cutter. Use a sharp knife to cut a curved line on it, so that it looks like the black markings on a penguin.

9 / Brush the bao bun with water, then position the black dough onto it. Use a tiny dot of black dough

for the eyes, then create the nose using a little of the orange dough. Place the finished bao bun on a small square of baking paper and place in a bamboo steamer. Cover lightly with plastic wrap or the steamer lid. Repeat (don't overcrowd the bao buns in the steamer, as they will rise).

10 / Leave the bao to rise for around 30 minutes (depending on the temperature of the room) until they are about 50 per cent bigger than before.

11 / Steam for 10 minutes over a low heat, then turn off the heat and leave in the steamer for 5 minutes before removing the lid. Serve straight away!

Tip: The mincemeat makes a very large quantity and can be decanted into sterilized jars to be used on future occasions. Alternatively, you can use storebought mincemeat – just add a finely chopped apple and the grated zest of a lemon and an orange to it to lighten the texture and improve the flavour.

Semlor Polar Bear Buns

In Sweden, semlor buns are usually served right after Christmas in the run-up to Lent, but this is a Christmas version of the traditional cream-filled yeasted bun, and as they're so tasty they deserve to be eaten more often. These buns are so adorable you won't be able to bear eating them, but at the same time they are delectable, so it's sure to be a *polarizing* decision. If you don't have time to make the almond paste, then use storebought marzipan instead.

MAKES: 16–20

DOUGH

120ml [½ cup] milk (use plant-based milk to make vegan)

50g [3½ Tbsp] butter (use dairy-free butter to make vegan)

120ml [½ cup] water

1 large egg (replace with 2 Tbsp aquafaba and 1 Tbsp vegetable oil to make vegan)

65g [⅓ cup] caster or granulated sugar

500g [3½ cups] strong white flour, plus extra for dusting

1½ tsp ground cardamom (for the best flavour, use fresh cardamom seeds, ground to a fine powder)

1 tsp salt

7g [2¼ tsp] fast-action dried [active dry] yeast

oil, for oiling

ALMOND PASTE/ MARZIPAN FILLING

125g [¾ cup plus 2 Tbsp] icing [confectioners'] sugar

125g [1¼ cups] ground almonds

1 egg white (or 40g [2⅔ Tbsp] aquafaba to make vegan)

¼ tsp almond extract

¾ tsp amaretto (optional)

CREAM FILLING

500ml [2 cups plus 2 Tbsp] double [heavy] cream

125g [¾ cup plus 2 Tbsp] icing [confectioners'] sugar

1 tsp vanilla bean paste

Tip: Use soy whipping cream to make the cream filling vegan.

PLUS

extra egg (or 4 parts plant-based milk to 1 part golden [light corn] syrup) to brush on top before baking

TO DECORATE

16–20 strawberries, halved

grey fondant

½ quantity of Royal Icing (page 16)

black gel food dye

1 / Heat the milk in the microwave until tepid, then melt the butter. Add all the wet ingredients to a large bowl or stand mixer and whisk together. Add the caster sugar and whisk again to combine, then add the flour, cardamom, salt and yeast (on opposite sides of bowl to the salt). If using a stand mixer, just attach the dough hook and let the machine knead for 8 minutes, or until the dough is smooth and elastic. If working by hand, first use a spoon to stir the wet and dry ingredients together until it comes together into a rough ball of dough, then turn the dough out onto a floured work surface and knead by hand until it is smooth and elastic.

2 / Place the dough in a lightly oiled bowl and cover with lightly oiled plastic wrap. Leave to rise at room temperature for 1–2½ hours until about doubled in size. The time for this will vary depending on the temperature of the room. Line a baking sheet with baking paper and set aside.

3 / When the dough has risen, divide it into individual balls, each one about 45–50g [1½–1¾oz]. Use your hands to shape each one so that it is smooth and taut on top, by stretching the dough and tucking it neatly underneath. Place on the prepared baking sheet and cover with lightly oiled plastic wrap. Leave to prove for 1 hour, or until almost doubled in size and when pressed with a finger the indent slowly comes back up halfway. Preheat the oven to 180°C [350°F/Gas mark 4] halfway through the rising time of the buns.

4 / When the buns have risen, brush with beaten egg (or to make vegan, 4 parts plant-based milk to 1 part golden syrup) and bake for 15–20 minutes until deep golden brown on top. Transfer to a wire rack and leave to cool completely.

5 / Meanwhile, make the almond paste. Stir the icing sugar and ground almonds together in a large bowl. Add the egg white (or aquafaba), almond extract and amaretto, if using, and stir together until it forms a paste. Set aside for now.

6 / When the buns are cool, whip the double cream (or use soy whipping cream) with the icing sugar and vanilla bean paste to soft peaks. Transfer the majority of the cream to a large piping [pastry] bag and cut a large opening. Transfer the remaining cream to a small piping bag and cut a small opening.

7 / Cut the tops of the buns off and scoop out 2 tsp of the insides. Spoon 1 tsp of the almond paste into the bottom of each bun, then use the large piping bag to pipe cream into the bun. Top with a strawberry (use the bottom end) to look like a Christmas hat. Shape a small piece of grey fondant and place it on the cream to represent a polar bear's nose area.

8 / Next, make the Royal Icing (page 16), then stir in enough black food dye to achieve the right colour. Transfer to a piping bag and cut a very small tip. Use this to add the polar bear's eyes and nose. Use the smaller piping bag of cream to add the polar bear's paws and a dot to the end of the Christmas hat. Repeat with all the buns.

"The bear-iers to your goals aren't always as big as you perceive them to be."

Stollen

I have recommended my favourite dried fruits and nuts to add to the dough below, but I also love the fact that this recipe can be flexible so you can use up packs of fruits or nuts that you might have lying around. You can substitute in different quantities of different ingredients, but just keep the weight of the total fruit and nuts similar. Dried apricots work well, as do pecans, currants and sultanas [golden raisins].

The stollen dough is quite wet and difficult to handle due to the quantity of butter (which is also what makes it so delicious!). Ideally, it is best to make this in a stand mixer with a dough hook attachment or a bread machine. Though if you're experienced with wet doughs, you can knead it by hand. You can get away with doing both rises in one day, but this bread has the best flavour if the first rise is done overnight in the fridge. This will also chill the butter and make it easier to shape in the morning. Be aware that this bread rises slowly due to the high quantity of milk, butter and dried fruit. It won't double in size like non-enriched doughs, but this is to be expected and is part of the beauty of the rich, dense and flavoursome stollen.

MAKES: 5 MINI STOLLEN

FRUIT MIX
150g [1 cup] raisins
50g [⅓ cup plus 2 tsp] dried cranberries
50g [⅓ cup] glacé [candied] cherries, roughly chopped
150g [1 cup plus 2 tsp] candied mixed peel
80g [⅔ cup] blanched almonds, roughly chopped
70ml [heaping 4 Tbsp] rum (use orange juice if you would like this to be non-alcoholic)

DOUGH
oil, for oiling
500g [3½ cups] strong white flour, plus extra for dusting
100g [½ cup] caster or granulated sugar
10g [1 Tbsp] fast-action dried [active dry] yeast
10g [2 tsp] salt
¾ tsp ground cinnamon
½ tsp ground cardamom
¼ tsp ground nutmeg
finely grated zest of 1 orange
finely grated zest of 1 lemon
200ml [¾ cup plus 2 Tbsp] whole milk
2 large eggs
150g [⅔ cup] unsalted softened butter, cubed
1 tsp vanilla bean paste

MARZIPAN MIDDLE
500g [3½ cups] icing [confectioners'] sugar, plus extra for dusting
500g [5 cups] ground almonds (the finer ground, the smoother the marzipan will be)
4 egg whites (about 140g [5oz])
1 tsp almond extract
3 tsp amaretto (optional)

Tip: You will have leftover marzipan if you are not decorating the outside of the stollen.

PLUS
50g [3½ Tbsp] butter, melted, for brushing
yellow food dye
3 Tbsp jam (ideally apricot), watered down a little
icing [confectioners'] sugar, for dusting
fondant in various colours (as pictured or create your own variation!)
2–4 fresh redcurrant sprigs (optional)
egg white (optional)
granulated sugar (optional)

1 / First, prepare the fruit mixture. Add all the dried fruit and nuts to a bowl, then pour over the rum. Leave to soak while you make the dough.

2 / For the dough, lightly oil a large bowl. Add the flour, sugar, yeast, salt (making sure this does not directly touch the yeast), ground spices and zest to a stand mixer bowl and stir together. Add the milk, eggs, softened butter and vanilla bean paste. Attach the dough hook and let the machine knead for 10 minutes, or until all the butter is mixed in and the dough is smooth and stretchy. Next, add the fruit mixture and knead in again until evenly distributed.

3 / Use a spatula to transfer the dough to the oiled bowl and cover with plastic wrap. Leave to rise overnight in the fridge (ideally), or you can leave it to rise for less time but at room temperature, until it is about 50 per cent bigger in size.

4 / Meanwhile, make the marzipan middle. Mix the dry ingredients in one bowl and, in a separate bowl, whisk together the wet ingredients. Add the wet to the dry and stir until just starting to combine. Lightly dust a work surface with a little icing sugar, then knead the marzipan until smooth, and form a ball. Wrap in plastic wrap until ready to use.

5 / When the dough has risen, line a large baking sheet with baking paper or a silicone mat. Tip the dough out onto a floured surface and knock out any air. Divide into 5 equal portions, then flatten each dough portion into a rectangle. Use about 40–50g [1½–1¾oz] marzipan per dough portion (reserving enough to decorate the outside of the stollen if you plan to do that) – rolling the marzipan into a log shape and placing in the centre of the dough. Wrap the dough around the marzipan and seal the edges. Place on the prepared baking sheet and loosely cover with plastic wrap, then leave to rise until the stollen are about 25 per cent bigger in size (they won't rise as much because the marzipan and dried fruit make up a lot of the dough), or until the dough slowly springs back about halfway when poked with a finger. Preheat the oven to 200°C [400°F/Gas mark 6] about 10 minutes before the dough has fully risen.

6 / Bake the dough for 10 minutes, then turn the oven down to 180°C [350°F/Gas mark 4] and bake for a further 20 minutes. You may need to cover the stollen with foil to stop them browning too much.

7 / When baked, brush with melted butter, then transfer to a wire rack to cool completely.

STEP 5 ▲

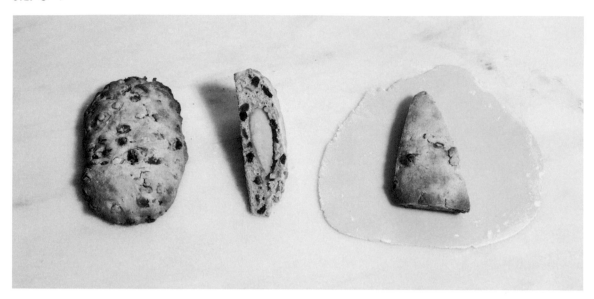

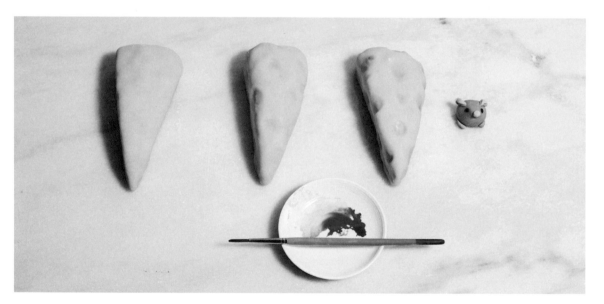

STEP 9 ▲

8 / When completely cool, you can either eat them or decorate them first before eating! To decorate, first knead a little yellow food dye into the remaining marzipan. Cut the long sides off each stollen, then slice the stollen diagonally in half. Brush the tops of the stollen all over with a little watered-down jam. Dust a work surface with a little icing sugar and roll out the marzipan.

9 / Drape pieces of marzipan over each stollen and shape it around the sides. Use a sharp knife to trim the excess marzipan, then create indents all over

the marzipan so it looks like cheese. Mix a little yellow food dye with water to create paint, and paint this into the indents to create a little colour definition.

10 / Shape some fondant mice in varied positions and holding chunks of marzipan 'cheese'. You can give the mice little Christmas hats, then make fondant holly. You can also create frosted redcurrants for additional decoration. Just brush with a little beaten egg white, then sprinkle with granulated sugar. Leave to dry for a few hours before using to decorate.

Soboro Turtle Bread

Not only are these adorable to look at, the sweet and nutty streusel topping contrasted with the super-soft cloud-like bread (thanks to the tangzhong!) will have you coming back for more. You can be creative with these, inventing your own little turtle characters.

MAKES: ABOUT 10

TANGZHONG
100ml [⅓ cup plus 1 Tbsp] water
25g [2¾ Tbsp] strong white flour

DOUGH
125ml [½ cup] whole milk (replace with plant-based milk to make vegan)
30g [2 Tbsp] unsalted butter (replace with dairy-free butter to make vegan)

oil, for oiling
10g [2½ tsp] caster or granulated sugar
1 tsp salt
1 large egg (replace with 2 Tbsp aquafaba and 1 Tbsp vegetable oil to make vegan)
350g [2½ cups] strong white flour, plus extra for dusting
7g [2¼ tsp] fast action dried [active dry] yeast

PLUS
1 egg, to brush on top before baking (or 4 parts plant-based milk to 1 part golden [light corn] syrup to make vegan)

STREUSEL TOPPING
75g [⅓ cup] butter (replace with dairy-free butter to make vegan)
50g [3½ Tbsp] peanut butter
90g [½ cup] light brown sugar

140g [1 cup] plain [all-purpose] flour
½ tsp baking powder

TO DECORATE (OPTIONAL)
edible black ink pen (or you can use black food dye mixed with a little water, then paint this on)
colourful sprinkles of your choice
hard pretzels
strawberries and cream or Royal Icing (optional)

1 / First, make the tangzhong. Using a balloon whisk, mix the water and flour together in a pan until smooth. Place the pan over a medium heat and stir constantly with a spatula until the mixture has thickened to a pudding-like consistency and it has reached 65°C [149°F]. Pour into a bowl, cover with plastic wrap (making sure it touches the surface of the tangzhong) and chill in the freezer for 10 minutes.

2 / Meanwhile, for the dough, warm the milk in the microwave. It should be warm but not hot. Melt the butter in the microwave. Lightly oil a large bowl.

3 / Place the milk and butter in another large bowl and add the sugar and salt. Add the chilled tangzhong to the bowl along with the egg (or aquafaba and oil) and whisk together.

4 / Add the flour and yeast to the mixture. If using a stand mixer, just allow the machine to knead for 10 minutes with the dough hook attachment. If working by hand, use a wooden spoon to combine everything into a shaggy ball of dough, then turn out onto a floured work surface and knead by hand for about 10–15 minutes. The dough will be sticky to start with, but avoid adding too much flour – it will gradually become less sticky as you knead it. If the dough sticks to the surface, use a dough scraper to scrape it off. Keep kneading until the dough is smooth; it will still be a little tacky but that is normal.

5 / Place the dough in the oiled bowl and cover with plastic wrap. Leave to rise at room temperature until about doubled in size. This takes about 1–2 hours, but it depends on the temperature of where you leave it.

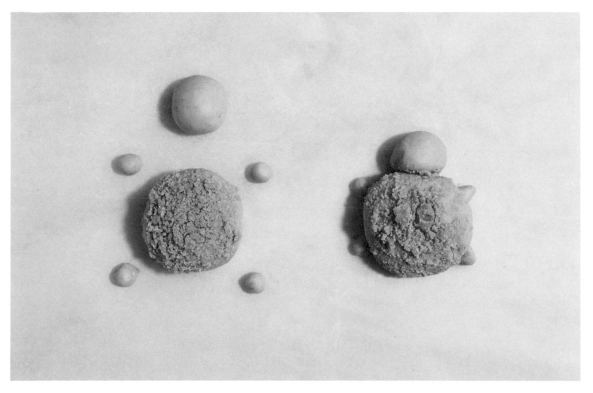

6 / When the dough has doubled in size, turn it out onto a lightly floured surface and knock back. Shape 9 balls of dough, each weighing 45g [1½oz], then shape them by tucking the dough under to create a smooth surface. These will form the main body of the turtle. There will be some leftover dough; this is to shape the head and legs later.

7 / Next, make the streusel topping. Cream the butter (or dairy-free butter), peanut butter and sugar together in a large bowl. Add the flour and baking powder and use your fingers to form a crumble.

8 / Brush the shaped bread dough pieces with a little water, then dip into the streusel to form a coating.

9 / Weigh out 10g [⅓oz] of dough for the head of the turtle, shape into a ball, then attach it to the body. Repeat for all 9 turtles. Shape the remaining dough into small balls and attach to the sides of the turtles to create feet.

10 / Cover the turtles with lightly oiled plastic wrap and leave to prove. The time this takes varies depending on the temperature of the location, but it won't be as long as the first rise. You are looking for the dough to have nearly doubled in size and spring back halfway when lightly indented with a finger. Fifteen minutes before the end of the rise, preheat the oven to 180°C [350°F/Gas mark 4].

11 / Whisk the egg (or plant-based milk plus golden syrup) in a small bowl, then brush this on top of the bread dough (avoiding the streusel topping). Bake for about 20 minutes, or until golden.

12 / Leave the turtles to cool completely on a wire rack, then add a face using an edible ink pen (or paint on black food dye mixed with a little water) and decorate with colourful sprinkles and pretzels for antlers. To create the hats, cut the narrower end off a strawberry, then pipe cream (or Royal Icing, page 16 if not eating immediately) onto the turtle's head. Place the strawberry hat on top of the cream, then top with a little blob of cream for the pom-pom.

"Shell-ebrate what you're good at!"

Little Treats

Reindeer Bakewell Tarts

These are the real deer!! Buttery and crisp pastry, fruity jam, moist almond frangipane and sweet icing topped with an even sweeter reindeer design. The trick with these is to make sure your pastry is elegantly thin, and blind baking is a must. Be careful not to overwork the pastry, and take this recipe one step at a time, as all will be right as rein.

MAKES: ABOUT 12

PASTRY
150g [⅔ cup] salted butter, at room temperature, plus extra for greasing
225g [1¾ cups] plain [all-purpose] flour (to make gluten free, use gluten-free flour plus ½ tsp xanthan gum), plus extra for dusting
40g [3¼ Tbsp] caster or granulated sugar
1 medium egg

FRANGIPANE
100g [½ cup] caster or granulated sugar
100g [7 Tbsp] unsalted butter, at room temperature
1 medium egg
¾ tsp almond extract
100g [1 cup] ground almonds

ICING
200g [1½ cups] icing [confectioners'] sugar, plus extra to thicken
2 Tbsp water

PLUS
4 Tbsp jam of your choice
black food dye
12 glacé [candied] cherries
24 hard pretzels

1 / First, make the pastry. Grease a 12-hole muffin tray with butter. Add the flour (or gluten-free flour plus xanthan gum) to a large bowl. Chop the butter and add it to the bowl, then rub it into the flour until it resembles fine breadcrumbs. Don't overwork. Stir in the caster sugar. Beat the egg in a separate small bowl, then add 2 Tbsp to the main mixing bowl and stir, gradually combining it with the rest of the mixture. When the egg is stirred through, use your hands to form the pastry into a ball.

2 / Roll out the pastry on a generously floured work surface as thinly as you can and use round cutters to stamp out 12 circles of pastry. Use your fingers to gently guide each circle of pastry into each muffin hole. Prick the bases with a fork 2–3 times, then place in the fridge to chill for 20 minutes. At this point, preheat the oven to 180°C [350°F/Gas mark 4].

3 / Line the chilled pastry shells with muffin or cupcake paper cases, then fill with baking beads (or you can use lentils or rice) and blind bake for about 15 minutes. Remove the baking beads and paper, then bake for a further 5–7 minutes until golden and crisp.

> Tip: I used a cupcake tray in which each hole is 7.5cm [3in] across, so I used a 10-cm [4-in] cutter for the bases and a 7.5-cm [3-in] one for the lids, but if you have a larger tray, then use larger cutters.

4 / Meanwhile, make the frangipane. Cream the sugar and butter together in a stand mixer (or use a handheld electric whisk) on high speed until light and fluffy. Add the egg and almond extract and mix until just combined. Fold in the ground almonds. Set aside.

5 / When the pastry has finished blind baking, remove the pastry cases from the muffin tray and place on a baking sheet; they should stand up on their own.

6 / Spoon 1 tsp of jam into each of the bases, then fill with frangipane, about three-quarters of the way up, as it will rise slightly. Return to the oven to bake for a further 15–20 minutes until the frangipane is set.

7 / When baked, transfer to a wire rack and leave to cool completely.

8 / Meanwhile, make the icing [frosting]. Just whisk the icing sugar and water together in a bowl until smooth. Spoon about 1 Tbsp into a separate bowl and add black food dye to colour, plus extra icing sugar to thicken to a pipeable consistency. Transfer to a piping [pastry] bag, ready for later. Cover the bowl of white icing with plastic wrap.

9 / When the tarts are cool, spoon the white icing over the top and carefully spread to the edges. Place a glacé cherry in the centre, then add the pretzel antlers. Cut a small tip off the black icing piping bag, then use to add eyes and a mouth. Use the back of a spoon to add a dot of white icing to the cherry nose to give it depth.

Vegan Alternative

PASTRY
360g [2¾ cups] plain [all-purpose] flour (or substitute with gluten-free flour plus ¾ tsp xanthan gum)
½ tsp salt
20g [1½ Tbsp] caster or granulated sugar
215g [1 cup minus 1 tsp] organic extra virgin coconut oil (not liquid, it should be at room temperature and scoopable)
65–80ml [4⅓–5 Tbsp] cold water

FRANGIPANE
50ml [3½ Tbsp] vegetable oil
75g [6 Tbsp] caster or granulated sugar
75g [¾ cup] ground almonds
50g [6 Tbsp] plain [all-purpose] flour
pinch of baking powder
50ml [3½ Tbsp] plant-based milk
¾ tsp almond extract

1 / To make the pastry, mix the dry ingredients together in a large bowl. Add the coconut oil and use your fingers to rub it in until it resembles fine breadcrumbs. Add enough water to combine and form into a ball. Use in the same way as the non-vegan pastry in the original recipe.

2 / For the frangipane, whisk the oil and sugar together in a large bowl. Add the ground almonds, flour and baking powder and whisk again until combined. Add the plant milk and almond extract and whisk. Use in the same way as the non-vegan frangipane in the original recipe.

"Deer to be different!"

Melting Snowman Cake Pops

These are fun to make! The great thing about them is that they last a good while, as the buttercream keeps the cake very moist, and it is all sealed in with a thin layer of chocolate. If you want to decorate these cake pops in a rush, you can always keep them plain and scatter sprinkles on before the chocolate sets – simple but still effective. You will need some cake-pop sticks. See page 82 for the alternative vegan recipe.

MAKES: 12–16

CAKE
100g [7 Tbsp] salted butter, at room temperature, plus extra for greasing
100g [½ cup] caster or granulated sugar
1 tsp vanilla bean paste
100g [3½oz] eggs (about 2 eggs)
130g [1 cup] self-raising flour (to make gluten free, substitute with gluten-free flour, ½ tsp xanthan gum and ¾ tsp baking powder)
1–2 Tbsp whole milk

BUTTERCREAM
70g [⅓ cup minus 1 tsp] salted butter at room temperature
140g [1 cup] icing [confectioners'] sugar
1 tsp vanilla bean paste
1–2 Tbsp whole milk

COATING
400g [14oz] white chocolate (ideally temper this first, see page 114, though it will work without – it just won't be as snappy)
white food dye (must be oil based and chocolate safe)
OR
300g [10½oz] white candy melts or compound chocolate (these don't need tempering, so will just set firm with a good snap, but they don't taste as good as real white chocolate!)

Tip: You will have some chocolate leftover from the coating, but it's a lot easier to temper a larger quantity, and you can always re-melt and use the chocolate later.

TO DECORATE
sprinkles
hard pretzels
½ quantity Royal Icing (page 16)
black and orange food dyes (or edible ink pens)
sweets [candies] or chocolate

1 / First, make the cake. Preheat the oven to 170°C [340°F/Gas mark 3]. Grease and line the base of an 18-cm [7-in] round cake tin with baking paper.

2 / Cream the butter and sugar together in a stand mixer (or use a handheld electric whisk) fitted with a balloon whisk attachment until light and fluffy, then whisk in the vanilla bean paste. Whisk the eggs in a separate bowl, then gradually add to the butter and sugar mix, whisking well after each addition.

3 / Add the self-raising flour (or gluten-free mixture) and whisk until just combined. Add the milk and whisk to soften the consistency.

4 / Spoon the batter into the prepared tin and bake for 15–20 minutes until a knife inserted into the centre comes out clean. Turn out onto a wire rack, remove the baking paper and leave to cool completely.

5 / Meanwhile, make the buttercream. Cream the butter and icing sugar together in a bowl until light in colour and fluffy. And the vanilla and milk and whisk again until the consistency is softer.

6 / When the cake is cool, remove any thick crusts, then use your hands to crumble the cake until it resembles breadcrumbs. Add the buttercream and whisk until well combined.

7 / Use the palms of your hands to shape the mixture into balls (about 30g [1oz] each). Try to make sure they are as smooth and round as possible. Place on a baking sheet and chill in the fridge for 2 hours, or until very firm.

8 / Next, melt the white chocolate (and stir in some white food dye to colour [optional]), or use white candy melts. You can melt the chocolate/ candy melts in the microwave in short 20-second bursts, stirring well in between, or you can put the chocolate/candy melts in a heatproof bowl and set the bowl over a pan of gently simmering water, making sure the base of the bowl doesn't touch the water.

9 / Dip the end of a cake pop stick into the chocolate (about 1cm [½in]), then stick this into the base of a cake ball. Repeat for all the balls, then leave to set for about 10 minutes.

10 / Temper the white chocolate (page 114), if using, or re-melt the candy melts. Dip each cake pop into the chocolate, covering the whole surface of the cake. Drizzle a little pool of chocolate onto baking paper, then place the cake pop onto this.

11 / While the chocolate is still soft, add the sprinkles to represent the snowmen's buttons, then add pretzel sticks for arms. You can position these at different angles, then leave to stand for about 20 minutes at room temperature, or until completely set.

12 / Once the chocolate coating is completely set, use black royal icing (or edible ink pen) to pipe eyes and dots for the mouth. Use an edible orange ink pen or royal icing dyed orange to add a triangle shape for the nose. Use a little leftover icing to stick on some sweets or chocolate for the hat. You can be creative with the hat and use whatever sweets and sprinkles you have lying around!

13 / Peel off the paper and eat straight away, or keep in the fridge and have as a treat days later (the chocolate layer keeps the cake inside very moist).

- LITTLE TREATS -

Vegan Alternative

WET INGREDIENTS
½ tsp white wine vinegar
140ml [½ cup plus 1 Tbsp] soy milk
55ml [¼ cup] sunflower oil (or other neutral-tasting oil)
½ Tbsp aquafaba (chickpea water)
1 tsp vanilla bean paste
pinch of salt

DRY INGREDIENTS
125g [1 cup minus 1 Tbsp] self-raising flour
95g [½ cup minus 1 tsp] caster or granulated sugar
½ Tbsp baking powder

VEGAN BUTTERCREAM
70g [⅓ cup] vegetable shortening
140g [1 cup] icing [confectioners'] sugar
1 tsp vanilla bean paste

1 / Follow step 1 of the original method, then make the vegan cake. In a large bowl, mix the vinegar with the soy milk until it curdles and thickens. Add the remaining wet ingredients and the salt and stir together.

2 / In a separate large bowl, combine all the dry ingredients. Add the dry ingredients to the wet and whisk until just combined. Pour straight away into the prepared cake tin and bake for 25–30 minutes until a knife inserted into the centre comes out clean.

3 / Turn the cake out onto a wire rack, remove the baking paper and leave to cool completely.

4 / Follow steps 5–13 in the original recipe, just omitting the milk from the buttercream (being careful not to overwhip), and using vegan white chocolate and vegan sweets or chocolate for the decoration.

"Snowbody's prrrfect."

White Chocolate, Raspberry and Gin Icebergs with Mini Penguins

Jaffa cakes can look a little fiddly, though it's mostly the spooning of the chocolate on top that can be tricky. Luckily, with the addition of the mini penguins, these jaffa cakes look more like miniature icebergs, which means you could probably get away with the chocolate being a little messier! If you don't want these to be alcoholic, just replace the gin with cold water.

MAKES: 24

JELLY
2 x 135-g [4¾-oz] packets of raspberry jelly cubes
200ml [¾ cup] hot water
90ml [6 Tbsp] gin

CAKE
butter, for greasing
2 large eggs
50g [¼ cup] caster or granulated sugar
60g [7¼ Tbsp] self-raising flour (to make gluten free, substitute with gluten-free flour plus ⅛ tsp xanthan gum

TOPPING
200g [7oz] white chocolate, chopped

PENGUINS
white, black and orange fondant
yellow sprinkles (star shaped or similar OR use yellow fondant)

1 / First make the jelly. Place the jelly cubes in a heatproof bowl and pour over the hot water. Stir until completely melted, then stir in the gin. Pour into a shallow tray (so the jelly is just under 1cm [½in] thick), then refrigerate for 1 hour, or until completely set.

2 / Next, make the cake. Preheat the oven to 170°C [340°F/Gas mark 3] and grease 2 x 12-hole cupcake trays with butter.

3 / In a large bowl, whisk the eggs and sugar together on high speed for 7 minutes. It should be pale, fluffy and hold a trail. Sift in the flour, then gently fold in to combine.

4 / Place about 1 Tbsp of cake batter into each cupcake hole and smooth the top. Bake for 8–10 minutes. You can tell they are ready when they have slightly pulled away from the sides.

5 / Leave to cool in the trays for 5 minutes before transferring to a wire rack and leaving until completely cool.

6 / Melt the white chocolate in a heatproof bowl set over a pan of gently simmering water, making sure the base of the bowl doesn't touch the water. Meanwhile, use a small round cutter (just a little smaller than the diameter of the cake) to stamp out jelly circles.

7 / If making the mini penguins, use the white fondant to create the main shape, then partially cover with a thin layer of black fondant, so it begins to look like a penguin. Use a little orange fondant for the nose and some black fondant for the eyes. You can use yellow fondant for the feet or use yellow star-shaped sprinkles or similar, sticking them on with a little melted chocolate.

8 / To assemble, place a jelly circle on top of each cooled cake, then use a spoon to carefully spread the white chocolate over the top, right to the edges. Try to avoid having the chocolate drip over the edges for a more traditional jaffa cake shape, but it doesn't matter if the chocolate does – the little penguins will detract from that! Leave to set.

Eggnog Mug Lattes

Cosy little eggnog lattes, and the best thing is that you can eat them in their entirety; cup and all! You and your friends and family will be eggstatic to get to eat these!

MAKES: 18–24

100g [7 Tbsp] butter,
   at room temperature,
   plus extra for greasing
60g [5 Tbsp] caster or
   granulated sugar
40g [3¼ Tbsp] light brown
   muscovado sugar
100g [3½oz] eggs (about
   2 medium eggs)
½ tsp ground nutmeg

¼ tsp ground cinnamon
140g [1 cup plus 1 Tbsp]
   self-raising flour
1 Tbsp sour cream

BRANDY SIMPLE SYRUP
20g [1 Tbsp plus 2 tsp]
   caster or granulated
   sugar
20ml [4 tsp] boiling water

10ml [2 tsp] brandy (omit if
   you would like this to be
   non-alcoholic)

CREAM
130ml [½ cup] double
   [heavy] cream
20g [2¼ Tbsp] icing
   [confectioners'] sugar
½ tsp vanilla bean paste

TO DECORATE
20–30g [2¼–3½ Tbsp] icing
   [confectioners'] sugar
hard pretzels
extra ground nutmeg,
   for sprinkling on top
mini marshmallows

1 / Preheat the oven to 180°C [350°F/Gas mark 4] and grease a mini-cupcake tray.

2 / Cream the butter and both sugars together in a large bowl until light in colour and fluffy. Whisk in the eggs, one at a time, beating well after each addition. Add the spices, flour and sour cream and whisk until just combined.

3 / Spoon the batter into the mini cupcake moulds, filling about three-quarters of the way up, as they will rise. Bake for 15 minutes, or until risen and springs back on top when touched with a finger.

4 / Meanwhile, make the brandy simple syrup. Stir the sugar and boiling water together in a heatproof bowl, then microwave in 30-second bursts, stirring after each, until all the sugar has dissolved. Add the brandy and stir together. Set aside for now.

5 / When the cakes have finished baking, leave to cool in the tray for 5 minutes, before removing and transferring to a wire rack to finish cooling.

6 / Once they're cool, place the icing sugar for decoration in a small bowl and stir in a tiny amount of water, a drop at a time, to make a paste. Use this to stick a hard pretzel (snap into shape first) to the side of each cake to make a handle.

7 / Next, whip the double cream with the icing sugar and vanilla bean paste together in a large bowl until you have soft peaks. Transfer to a piping [pastry] bag with an open star-shaped nozzle (or any similar) and pipe a little swirl on top of each cake. Finally, sprinkle or sift over a little nutmeg and top with a couple of mini marshmallows.

Tip: if you would like to make mini marshmallow creatures, such as pigs and seals, you will need mini marshmallows, royal icing dyed pink and a black edible ink pen or some royal icing dyed black.

Christmas Pudding Chocolate Orange Profiteroles

Chocolate choux pastry filled with silky smooth chocolate orange crème diplomate filling, and then topped with even more chocolate! These are irresistible, be warned. You will be eating one after another!

Tip: If you don't have the time or ingredients to make crème diplomate, you can fill these with whipped cream flavoured with a little icing sugar and orange zest. They will still be delicious!

MAKES: ABOUT 15

CHOUX PASTRY
55g [3¾ Tbsp] unsalted butter
150ml [⅔ cup] water
pinch of salt
30g [3¾ Tbsp] plain [all-purpose] flour
30g [3½ Tbsp] strong white flour (to make gluten free, swap both plain [all-purpose] and strong white flour for 60g [7¼ Tbsp] gluten-free flour

plus a pinch of xanthan gum)
2 medium eggs
10g [2 tsp] cocoa [unsweetened chocolate] powder

CHOCOLATE ORANGE CRÈME DIPLOMATE FILLING
300ml [1¼ cups] whole milk
¾ tsp vanilla bean paste

5 large egg yolks
100g [½ cup] caster or granulated sugar
finely grated zest of 1 orange
20g [4 tsp] cocoa [unsweetened chocolate] powder
45g [½ cup minus 1 tsp] cornflour [cornstarch]
125ml [½ cup] double [heavy] cream

TO DECORATE
icing [confectioners'] sugar, for dusting
green (about 80g [3oz]) and red (about 20g [¾oz]) fondant
100g [3½oz] white chocolate, roughly chopped
edible eyes
½ quantity Royal Icing (page 16)

1 / Preheat the oven to 200°C [400°F/Gas mark 6].

2 / To make the choux pastry, chop the butter and add it to a small saucepan with the water and salt. Heat until the butter has melted and the mixture is starting to bubble. Meanwhile, combine both flours in a separate bowl. When the butter mixture is bubbling, remove it from the heat and add the flours all in one go. Stir with a wooden spoon until it forms a smooth ball that pulls away from the sides very easily – this is called a panada.

3 / Transfer the panada to a stand mixer fitted with a paddle attachment (or use handheld electric beaters) and leave to cool for 5–10 minutes. You can mix it on low speed to help cool it down faster.

4 / Add one of the eggs to the panada, mixing on slow speed until combined. Whisk the second egg in a separate bowl and add gradually, 1 Tbsp at a time, mixing well after each addition. You are looking for a glossy consistency, which leaves a 'v' when a spoon is lifted out of the dough. Whisk in the cocoa powder.

5 / Transfer to a piping [pastry] bag and cut a medium tip. Line a large baking sheet with baking paper or a silicone mat, then pipe around 15 rounds onto the sheet. Dip your finger in water and use this to flatten the tip of each choux.

6 / Bake for 10 minutes then turn the oven down to 180°C [350°F/Gas mark 4] and bake for a further 20–25 minutes. Don't open the oven until at least 25 minutes have passed, to avoid the choux pastry deflating.

7 / When the choux have finished baking, immediately turn them over and use a knife to pierce the base. This is so that the air inside has somewhere to escape.

8 / While the choux are cooling, make the crème diplomate filling. Add the milk and vanilla bean paste to a medium saucepan and stir over a low–medium heat until just starting to bubble. Meanwhile, in a separate bowl, whisk the egg yolks and caster sugar until light and fluffy. Add the orange zest, cocoa powder and cornflour and mix until just combined. When the milk mixture is bubbling, pour a small amount (about one-third) into the egg yolk mixture, while whisking. When combined, add the rest of the milk while still whisking constantly, then pour it all back into the pan.

9 / Put the pan back over a medium heat and whisk by hand until the mixture is very thick. Switch to a spatula when it becomes too thick to whisk and use the spatula to get right into the edges of the pan. When the mixture is very thick, spoon into a shallow metal tray, cover with plastic wrap (making sure it

touches the surface of the crème pâtissière) and leave to cool in the fridge. If you have any lumps in your crème pat, then you can strain it before chilling.

10 / When the crème pâtissière is completely cool, whip the double cream until it forms soft peaks, then gently fold into the crème pâtissière. It may help to whisk the crème pat first just to loosen it a little. With the addition of the whipped cream to lighten it, you now have crème diplomate. Transfer this to a piping [pastry] bag and leave in the fridge until ready to use.

11 / Pipe the crème diplomate into the cooled choux buns through the hole created earlier, making sure each one is filled completely.

12 / Next, make the decorations. Dust a work surface with a little icing sugar, then roll out the green fondant. Use a small holly-shaped plunger cutter to stamp out 2 pieces of holly per choux bun. Roll small balls of red fondant between your fingers – make 3 per choux bun.

13 / Next, melt the chocolate. Place the white chocolate in a microwavable bowl and melt in short 20-second bursts in the microwave, stirring well between each.

14 / Use a spoon to carefully control drips around the top of each choux bun, then arrange the fondant decorations on top to make a Christmas pudding! Add edible eyes to some, using the royal icing to make them stick.

Irish Cream Snowmen Choux

Christmas isn't complete without choux pastry filled with the most delicious Irish cream filling... plus adorable snowmen too.

MAKES: 18–24

CHOUX PASTRY
85g [⅓ cup plus 2 tsp] unsalted butter
225ml [1 cup] water
pinch of salt
50g [6 Tbsp] plain [all-purpose] flour
50g [5¾ Tbsp] strong white flour (to make gluten free, swap both plain and strong white flour for 100g [¾ cup] gluten-free flour plus ¼ tsp xanthan gum)
2–3 medium eggs

IRISH CREAM LIQUEUR FILLING
480ml [2 cups plus 2 Tbsp] double [heavy] cream
4 Tbsp icing [confectioners'] sugar
1 Tbsp Irish cream liqueur

VANILLA ICING
200g [1½ cups minus 1 Tbsp] icing [confectioners'] sugar
40–50ml [2⅔–3½ Tbsp] water
½ tsp vanilla bean paste

PLUS
matchstick cookies or similar
sprinkles
½ quantity Royal Icing (page 16)
orange and black food dyes (or more sprinkles)
fondant, fruit, nuts, candy canes, etc. for additional decoration (optional)

1 / Preheat the oven to 200°C [400°F/Gas mark 6].

2 / To make the choux pastry, chop the butter and add it to a small saucepan with the water and salt. Heat until the butter has melted and the mixture is starting to bubble. Meanwhile, combine both flours (or gluten-free flour plus xanthan gum) in a separate bowl. When the butter mixture is bubbling, remove it from the heat and add the flours all in one go. Stir with a wooden spoon until it forms a smooth ball that pulls away from the sides very easily – this is called a panada.

3 / Transfer the panada to a stand mixer fitted with a paddle attachment (or use a handheld electric whisk) and leave to cool for 5–10 minutes.

4 / Add 2 eggs, one at a time, to the panada, mixing on slow speed after each addition until combined. Whisk a third egg in a separate bowl and gradually add 1 Tbsp at a time, mixing well after each addition. You may not need to add the third egg, or you may need to add a little or all of it. It's important to add it gradually to avoid having a batter that is too runny. You are looking for a glossy consistency, which leaves a 'v' when a spoon is lifted out of the dough.

5 / Transfer to a piping [pastry] bag and cut a medium tip. Line 2 baking sheets with baking paper or a silicone mat, then pipe 20 x 3-cm [1¼-in] circles onto one of the baking sheets.

6 / Bake in the oven for 10 minutes, then turn the oven down to 180°C [350°F/Gas mark 4] and bake for a further 20 minutes. Don't open the oven until at least 25 minutes have passed, to avoid the choux pastry deflating.

7 / Meanwhile, pipe a second batch onto the other baking sheet. This time you will need 20 x 2.5-cm [1-in] circles (there will be some leftover choux so you can pipe extra if you like).

8 / When the first batch of choux have finished baking, immediately turn them over and use a knife to pierce the base. This is so that the air inside has somewhere to escape, and also gives you a place to pipe in the filling. Bake the second batch of choux for 10 minutes at 200°C [400°F/Gas mark 6], then a further 10 minutes at 180°C [350°F/Gas mark 4].

9 / Meanwhile, make the Irish cream filling. Add all the ingredients to a clean, grease-free bowl and whip on medium-high speed until stiff enough to pipe and hold its shape. Don't overwhip. Transfer the whipped cream to a piping bag and cut a small tip.

10 / Pipe the cream into the cooled choux buns through the hole created earlier, making sure each one is filled completely.

11 / To make the icing [frosting], whisk all the ingredients together in a bowl, then spoon the icing over the top of each choux bun. Stack the smaller choux bun on top of the larger one.

12 / Decorate with matchstick cookie arms and sprinkles for buttons. These will stick if you add them before the icing sets but use a little extra if needed. Add the facial features with royal icing dyed black and orange, or use sprinkles. You can also use nuts, fondant or fruits to create accessories for their heads.

STEP 11 ▼

STEP 12 ▲

- LITTLE TREATS -

Yuzu Curd Santa Tartlets with Strawberries & Cream

These look cute, plus taste dreamy thanks to the combination of tangy curd, luscious cream and the sweetness from the strawberries. If you don't have yuzu, you can make these with lemon instead. If you don't have time to make the pastry then buy it ready-made.

MAKES: 6

PASTRY
125g [½ cup plus 1 Tbsp] slightly salted butter, at room temperature, plus extra for greasing
180g [1⅓ cups] plain [all-purpose] flour (for gluten free, substitute 180g [1⅓ cups] gluten-free flour plus ½ tsp xanthan gum), plus extra for dusting
30g [2½ Tbsp] caster or granulated sugar

1 medium egg

CURD
180ml [¾ cup] yuzu juice
2 Tbsp yuzu zest, very finely chopped
150g [⅔ cup] salted butter
2 large eggs
2 egg yolks
250g [1¼ cups] caster or granulated sugar

VEGAN CURD ALTERNATIVE
200ml [¾ cup plus 1 Tbsp] yuzu juice
2 Tbsp yuzu zest, very finely chopped
240g [1¼ cups] caster or granulated sugar
2½ Tbsp cornflour (cornstarch)
60ml [4 Tbsp] coconut milk
80g [⅓ cup plus 1 Tbsp] coconut oil

CREAM
150ml [⅔ cup] double [heavy] cream (to make vegan, use soy whip)
30g [3½ Tbsp] icing [confectioners'] sugar

PLUS
6–12 strawberries
black fondant and sprinkles

1 / Grease 6 x 10-cm [4-in] tart tins with butter.

2 / Add the flour (or gluten-free flour plus xanthan gum) to a large bowl. Chop the butter and add it to the bowl, then rub it into the flour until it resembles fine breadcrumbs. Don't overwork. Stir in the caster sugar. Beat the egg in a separate small bowl, then add 2 Tbsp to the main mixing bowl and stir, gradually combining it with the rest of the mixture. When the egg is stirred through, use your hands to form the pastry into a ball.

3 / Roll out pastry on a generously floured work surface. Using a 12-cm [4½-in] cutter, stamp out circles to line each of the tart tins. Guide the pastry into the shape of the tart tin, then trim off the top edges. Prick the base a few times with a fork.

4 / Place the tart shells in the fridge for 20 minutes, or the freezer for less time if you are in a rush. Preheat the oven to 180°C [350°F/Gas mark 4].

5 / Cover the tarts with foil, then fill with baking beads (or rice or lentils), making sure they go into all the edges and bake for 15 minutes with the foil on.

6 / Remove the foil and baking beads and bake for a further 5–10 minutes so that the pastry is golden brown. Remove from the tins and leave to cool while you make the curd filling.

7 / Add the yuzu juice, zest and butter to a pan and heat over a low heat until the butter has melted. In a separate bowl, whisk the eggs, egg yolks and sugar together. Pour about one-sixth of the hot fruit/butter mix onto the egg yolk mix, whisking constantly, then pour all of this back into the pan. Continue whisking over a medium heat until the curd is thick and it coats the back of a spoon. It will thicken a lot more after chilling in the fridge.

8 / If making the vegan curd, combine the juice, zest, sugar and cornflour in a small pan and stir constantly over a medium heat until the mixture has thickened and it coats the back of a spoon. Remove from the heat, then immediately add the coconut milk and coconut oil and stir in until completely melted and combined. Pour the mixture into a bowl, cover with plastic wrap (making sure it touches the surface of the curd to avoid it forming a film) and freeze for 1 hour. It won't seem very thick right now, but it will thicken to the perfect consistency as it cools.

9 / Spoon the curd into the tart shells, then place in the fridge to chill completely for at least 4 hours, or until firm.

10 / When the curd is firm and set, you can decorate the tarts. Whip the cream with the icing sugar in a large bowl until you have soft peaks. Transfer 2 Tbsp to a piping [pastry] bag and cut a small tip. Transfer the rest to a second piping bag and cut a medium tip. Slice the top off a strawberry, so that there is a wide flat base for it to stand up, then slice off the top third of the strawberry.

11 / Using the medium-tip piping bag, decoratively pipe whipped cream onto the curd (slightly wider than the base of a strawberry) and top with the strawberry base. Pipe whipped cream on top of this, then top with the smaller strawberry piece. Use the smaller-tip bag to pipe whipped cream to create buttons for the Santa and for the bobble on top of the hat. You can also add little arms, if you wish. You can then place the whole bag of whipped cream into another bag that has a decorative nozzle attachment and use to pipe Santa's beard. Add the eyes using black fondant (or sprinkles), and you can also top the hat with a sprinkle of your choice. You can add additional Santas, if you like!

Cheesecake Snow Globes

You can make edible clear snow globes using gelatine, but they aren't anything you would actually want to eat and take a little while to make, so it makes more sense to use a glass bowl for your snow globe! You can make these in advance, and friends and family will be impressed with your presentation. You can swirl various fillings through these cheesecakes, such as curd, jam, peanut butter, fresh berries, caramel, etc. and you can also create any creatures you like to live in the snow globe… pandas, penguins, foxes, cats, or maybe even model your friends or family!

There are a few different options for the cookie base and the cheesecake. The alternate cookie base is good if you are vegan and gluten free, though is noticeably different to your ordinary cheesecake base (but still delicious!). The baked vegan filling is similar tasting to the dairy-based baked cheesecake, whereas the raw vegan filling is decadent and delicious in its own way (some people prefer it!), but different. You will need ramekins and glass bowls which fit neatly on top.

MAKES: 6–8 MINI CHEESECAKES

BASE
250g [9oz] digestive biscuits [graham crackers] (or use vegan/gluten-free storebought or homemade cookies, such as Speculoos, page 12)
100g [7 Tbsp] melted butter (or use the same quantity of melted vegan butter, or 80g [scant ¼ cup] melted coconut oil)

ALTERNATE BASE (VEGAN AND GLUTEN FREE)
150g [¾ cup] dates
150g [1 cup] blanched almonds (you can substitute other nuts and adjust quantities for desired sweetness)

pinch of salt
20g [heaping 1 Tbsp] coconut oil

FILLING
300g [1¼ cups] cream cheese
150ml [⅔ cup] double [heavy] cream
150g [⅔ cup] mascarpone cheese
100g [½ cup] caster or granulated sugar
finely grated zest of 1 lemon

VEGAN FILLING
180g [1⅓ cups] cashews
grated zest and juice of 1 lemon
60g [5 Tbsp] coconut oil, melted
150ml [⅔ cup] coconut milk

120g [⅓ cup plus 4 tsp] agave syrup or golden [light corn] syrup or similar

VEGAN FILLING OPTION 2 (BAKED)
300g [10½oz] silken tofu
260g [1 cup plus 1 Tbsp] vegan cream cheese
1½ Tbsp cornflour [cornstarch]
135g [½ cup plus 2 Tbsp] caster or granulated sugar
1¼ Tbsp coconut oil, melted
finely grated zest of 2 lemons

TO DECORATE
fondant
icing sugar, to dust (optional)

1 / First make the base. Put the biscuits into a plastic food bag, seal, then use a rolling pin to crush the biscuits into fine crumbs. Transfer to a bowl, then pour over the melted butter (or vegan butter). Stir until all the crumbs are well coated, then press into the bases of 6–8 ramekins to create an even and compact layer. Chill in the fridge for 1–2 hours to set. Alternatively, you can make the vegan and gluten-free version. Blitz the dates in a food processor until sticky and forms a ball. Add the almonds, salt and coconut oil and process again until combined. Press into the ramekins and chill in the same way.

2 / For the filling, just whisk all the ingredients together in a bowl until combined. For the vegan no-bake alternative, first soak the cashews by pouring over boiling water and leaving for 30 minutes, then draining all the water. Blitz the cashews, lemon zest and juice in a food processor until smooth. Add the melted coconut oil, coconut milk and agave syrup and process again until very smooth. Spoon either filling over the chilled base in each ramekin (and at this point you can swirl any desired filling through – try peanut butter, jam, fresh berries, chocolate, curd, etc.) and chill in the fridge for 4–6 hours until completely set. For the baked vegan alternative,

preheat the oven to 160°C [325°F/Gas mark 3]. Use a food processor to blend the tofu until smooth, then add the cream cheese and blend again. Remove 2 Tbsp and whisk this together with the cornflour in a separate bowl. Add back to the main mixture, along with the caster sugar, melted coconut oil and grated lemon zest. Mix together again until smooth and combined. Spoon over the chilled base, then bake for about 30 minutes. It should be slightly browned on top, but still have a little wobble in the centre. After baking, chill in the fridge for at least 6 hours, or until firm.

3 / When the cheesecake is set, decorate with fondant creatures, then top with the glass bowl. Dust with icing sugar, if you like.

> Tip: You can decorate with any fondant creatures you like. For the cat, shape some white fondant into a cat, then paint it with a little food dye mixed with a little water or alcohol.

Hedgehog German Cookies

Festive little hedgehogs! These German-style cookies are extremely delicate and have a 'melt in your mouth' texture thanks to the addition of potato starch. You can replace the potato starch with plain [all-purpose] flour, but this will result in a more ordinary shortbread, rather than the special texture of these cookies. Feel free to decorate these hedgehogs with whatever sprinkles you like!

MAKES: 15–20

125g [½ cup plus 1 Tbsp] salted butter, at room temperature, cubed
40g [5 Tbsp] icing [confectioners'] sugar
½ tsp vanilla bean paste
125g [¾ cup plus 1 Tbsp] potato starch, plus extra

for dusting if needed
80g [⅔ cup minus 1 Tbsp] plain [all-purpose] flour (to make gluten free, substitute with gluten-free flour plus ½ tsp xanthan gum)

PLUS
150g [5oz] dark [bittersweet] chocolate, roughly chopped
hard pretzels
festive sprinkles of your choice
brown round sprinkles

1 / Cream the butter and icing sugar together in a stand mixer (or use a handheld electric whisk) fitted with a balloon whisk attachment until light and fluffy. Add the vanilla bean paste and mix again until combined. Sift in the potato starch and plain flour (or gluten-free flour plus xanthan gum), then combine into a ball using a spatula. Avoid overmixing.

2 / Shape the dough into smooth round balls (about 19–26g [¾–1oz] each) between your hands. Refine the shape further by making one end narrower than the other and try to shape a smaller point for where the hedgehog's nose will be. The dough is a little sticky and tricky to handle, so use potato starch or flour to stop it sticking to your hands. Try to handle the dough lightly and, the less you handle it, the more the cookies will crumble and melt in your mouth.

3 / Line a baking sheet with baking paper. Place the cookies on the sheet and chill in the fridge for 15–30 minutes. At this point, preheat the oven to 160°C [325°F/Gas mark 3].

4 / Bake for about 15–20 minutes (smaller pieces will bake quicker). They will expand slightly but will hold their shape very well.

5 / When baked, leave to cool for 5 minutes on the baking sheet, then transfer carefully to a wire rack to let them cool completely (be careful when transferring as the cookies are very fragile – though this is also part of what makes them so delicious too).

6 / Place the dark chocolate in a microwaveable bowl and melt in short 20-second bursts in the microwave, stirring well between each.

7 / Spoon the chocolate over the cookies, leaving the face exposed and reserving some of the chocolate for the facial features. Break the pretzel sticks so that they look like reindeer antlers. Stick the antlers on either side of the hedgehog's head, pressing slightly into the cookie so they stay in place. Scatter sprinkles over so they stick to the chocolate. Repeat with all the hedgehog cookies.

8 / Use a spatula to transfer the remaining chocolate to a piping [pastry] bag and cut a very small tip. Pipe a little chocolate to adhere a round brown sprinkle for the hedgehog's nose, then pipe 2 dots of chocolate for the eyes.

Robin Cookies

Need a cute and easy-to-do Christmas cookie? Look no feather. The only tricky part of this recipe is the sugar glass centre, but if you don't fancy this, you can leave the middle empty, or sandwich together two cookies like the Arctic Fox Cookies recipe on page 118.

MAKES: 12

COOKIE DOUGH

1 quantity Speculoos dough (page 12 – you can also add the finely grated zest of 2 lemons or 2 oranges to flavour)

plain [all-purpose] flour, for dusting

SUGAR CENTRE

225g [1 cup plus 2 Tbsp] caster or granulated sugar

150g [⅔ cup] liquid glucose

50ml [3½ Tbsp] water

orange gel food dye

PLUS

1 quantity Royal Icing (page 16; use aquafaba instead of the egg white for vegan royal icing)

black and orange gel food dyes

sprinkles of your choice

1 / Line a baking sheet that you can fit in the fridge with baking paper. Make the dough by following the recipe on page 12.

2 / Roll out the dough on a lightly floured work surface, then use cutters to stamp out circles, about 7.5cm [3in] in diameter, and transfer to the prepared baking sheet. On half the cookies, stamp out a smaller circle, about 4cm [1½in] from the lower third area (refer to the photo for guidance).

3 / Bake and leave to cool as specified on page 12.

4 / When the cookies are cool, make the sugar glass for the centre. Add the caster sugar, liquid glucose and water to a small saucepan and stir to combine. Add a drop of orange gel food dye to colour. Heat over a high heat, but don't stir at all until the mixture reaches 150°C [300°F]. Remove the pan from the heat and use a large spoon to spoon the sugar syrup into the centre of the cookies. Immediately scatter

over sprinkles. Leave the sugar syrup for 20 minutes, or until completely hardened, then peel off the baking paper.

5 / Next, make the Royal Icing (page 16). Spoon one-third of the mixture into a piping [pastry] bag, then divide the remaining icing between 2 bowls. Stir black food dye into one bowl and orange food dye into the other to colour. Transfer each colour to a piping bag and cut a small opening on each. Use to pipe a robin design (refer to the photo for guidance). The wings are an optional extra decoration. You can make them by letting the leftover sugar syrup (used for the centres) cool, then pulling it into a long wide ribbon using your hands and cutting it into pieces with scissors. Just be careful not to do this when the sugar is too hot! It needs to be cooled to the point where it can be stretched and is malleable. It's not a problem if this doesn't work for you, as the robins still look good without the wings!

Festive Bunny Madeleines

Bunnies aren't just for Easter; they can be festive too! You will love these madeleines, as they are beautifully soft and light, and unlike other madeleine recipes, you don't need to wait for the batter to rest overnight. There's sure to be a *furry* for all to eat these, so you better hop to it!

MAKES: 12

MADELEINES

100g [½ cup] caster or
  granulated sugar
2 medium eggs
70g [⅓ cup minus 1 tsp]
  salted butter, plus extra
  for greasing
135g [1 cup] plain
  [all-purpose] flour
  (to make gluten free,
  substitute with gluten-
  free flour plus ¼ tsp
  xanthan gum)
1 tsp baking powder
30ml [2 Tbsp] whole milk
finely grated zest of
  1 lemon

VEGAN MADELEINE VERSION

125g [1 cup minus 1 Tbsp]
  plain [all-purpose] flour
  (to make gluten free,
  substitute with gluten-
  free flour plus ¼ tsp
  xanthan gum)
4 Tbsp cornflour
  [cornstarch]
1¼ tsp baking powder
100g [½ cup] caster or
  granulated sugar
125ml [½ cup] soy milk
3 Tbsp vegetable oil
finely grated zest of
  1 lemon

ROSE DIP

40–45ml [3 Tbsp] water
200g [1½ cups
  minus 1 Tbsp] icing
  [confectioners'] sugar,
  plus extra for piping
⅛ tsp rosewater, or to taste
pink, black and red food
  dyes

PLUS

icing [confectioners']
  sugar, for rolling out
green and red fondant

"Things might be a little lopsided, but that's what makes it unique."

1 / Make the madeleines. Add the sugar and eggs to a large bowl (ideally a stand mixer) and whisk on high speed for 7 minutes, or until the batter is thick and holds a trail. Meanwhile, melt the butter in the microwave in very short bursts so that it is liquid but not too hot. Put the flour and baking powder in a separate bowl.

2 / Pour the milk into the batter, then sift in the flour and baking powder. Add the lemon zest and whisk until just incorporated. Pour in the cooled, melted butter and whisk until just combined. Do not overmix.

3 / Cover with plastic wrap and freeze for 30 minutes. Melt a little extra butter and use this to grease a madeleine tin. Freeze the madeleine tin too. At this point, preheat the oven to 220°C [425°F/Gas mark 7].

4 / Transfer the chilled batter to a piping bag. Snip a medium tip and pipe 12–15 blobs into the chilled mould. Place in the oven and immediately reduce the temperature to 200°C [400°F/Gas mark 6]. Bake for 8–12 minutes until each madeleine has a hump and is starting to colour at the edges. When baked, slide them out of the mould and onto a rack.

5 / Meanwhile, make the rose dip. Whisk the water and icing sugar together in a bowl until smooth and runny but still opaque when coating the back of

a spoon. Add the rosewater to flavour. Pour into a wide-brimmed cup (choose one suitable for dipping the madeleines into) and cover with plastic wrap.

6 / When the madeleines are cool, dip one by one (narrow, scalloped end first) into the rose dip. Aim to have just under half of the madeleine's surface area covered. Leave to set on a wire rack.

7 / You will have leftover rose dip. While the madeleines set, stir extra icing sugar into the dip so it is more pipeable, then divide it between 3 bowls. Stir in the red food dye to one bowl, then the black dye to another (for light grey) and leave the third bowl white. Transfer the icings to 3 piping [pastry] bags and cut a small tip. Use the white icing to pipe ears, then leave to set. When it has set, use the red icing to fill in the ears and pipe eyes and a nose, and use the grey icing to pipe the eyebrows and mouth.

8 / Dust a surface with icing sugar and roll out a very small amount of green fondant. Use plunger cutters to stamp out mini pieces of holly. Decorate the bunnies with the holly plus small balls of red fondant. Use leftover icing to make them stick.

FOR THE VEGAN ALTERNATIVE
Whisk together all the ingredients, then follow steps 3–8 of the original recipe.

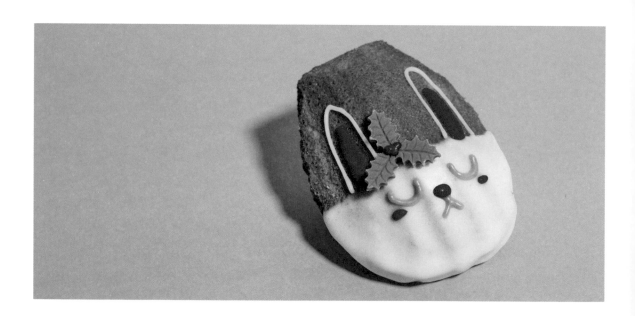

Canelé Christmas Trolls

In Iceland, Santa is not a big part of Christmas celebrations – instead there are 13 troll-like Yule lads and an evil Christmas cat. They give gifts for those who have been nice and leave potatoes in shoes for those who have been naughty. Each troll has its own personality and behaves in a slightly different manner. Decorate these canelés so that each represents a troll, using your own imagination!

It's best to make the batter for these in advance for the best flavour and texture, though I have made some the same day and they are still delicious! This batter takes 10 minutes to make, and the best thing is that you can leave the batter in the fridge and just bake a small, fresh batch every couple of days. Be warned that if you choose to use the beeswax, it can be very messy, as it will instantly harden and cling to anything it lands on, plus beeswax is an ingredient that you will likely just use for canelés and nothing else. BUT it is worth it if you grow to love making canelés as much as I do. However, to start with, try greasing with butter and using cheaper canelé moulds; they will still taste incredible – custardy on the inside and crisper and caramelized on the outside. They are best eaten the same day.

MAKES: 12–14

500ml [2 cups plus 2 Tbsp] whole milk
1 Tbsp vanilla bean paste (or 2 vanilla pods [beans])
200g [1 cup] caster or granulated sugar
2 medium eggs
2 medium egg yolks
50g [3½ Tbsp] salted butter, melted, plus extra butter or plant-based butter (or 60 per cent beeswax and 40 per cent butter), for greasing
100g [¾ cup minus ½ Tbsp] strong white bread flour (to make gluten free, substitute with gluten-free flour plus ¼ tsp xanthan gum)
3½ Tbsp rum

ICING
100g [¾ cup minus ½ Tbsp] icing [confectioners'] sugar, plus extra to adjust consistency
20ml [4 tsp] water, plus extra to adjust consistency

WHIPPED CREAM
100ml [⅓ cup plus 1 Tbsp] double [heavy] cream
20g [2¼ Tbsp] icing [confectioners'] sugar
food dyes

TO DECORATE
sprinkles
edible eyes
edible gold and silver paint
hard pretzels
matchsticks or pocky

1 / Add the milk and vanilla to a small pan and heat until starting to simmer, then turn off the heat and leave to cool for about 3 minutes.

2 / Meanwhile, whisk the sugar, eggs and egg yolks together in a large bowl. Melt the butter in the microwave for about 15 seconds, then whisk into the sugar and eggs until combined.

3 / Put the flour (or gluten-free flour plus xanthan gum) in a separate bowl. Add one-quarter of the milk mixture to the eggs and whisk in. Add one-quarter of the flour and keep whisking. Keep alternating and mixing well until everything is incorporated. Finally, add the rum and whisk again. Cover the bowl with plastic wrap, then chill in the fridge for at least 24 hours.

4 / When you're ready to bake, preheat the oven to 250°C [500°F/Gas mark 10], then coat your moulds. You can use any type of mould, but copper ones will give the best results. If using silicone or metal moulds, just coat with a little butter. You can use just butter in the copper moulds too, though the canelés will have a shinier crust and slide out more easily if you use a 60 per cent beeswax and 40 per cent butter mixture, all melted together (just melt in short bursts in the microwave). In order to get a thin and even coating, pour the mixture into the mould, then pour it straight back out.

5 / Fill the moulds with the batter, about 1cm [½in] from the top, and bake for 10 minutes, then turn the oven down to 180°C [350°F/Gas mark 4] and bake for a further 45 minutes. The canelés should be a very deep, dark and a caramelized brown colour on top.

6 / Remove from the moulds straight away, tapping if they are a little resistant to come out. Place on a wire rack to cool.

7 / To make the icing [frosting], whisk the icing sugar and water together in a bowl. Whip the cream with the icing sugar in a separate bowl until soft peaks form. Once the canelés are cool, you can decorate each one in a different way to create your Christmas trolls. Pipe cream on top and decorate like a Christmas tree. Try adding icing drips down the side. You can add sprinkles and eyes to these to decorate or paint them once set. Stick in pretzels, matchsticks or pocky for arms and ears. Have fun and see what you can come up with!

Vegan Alternative

The crust turns out a little thicker, but it still tastes silky and custardy inside.

500ml [2 cups] soy milk
200g [1 cup] caster or granulated sugar
60g [⅓ cup] strong white flour (or gluten-free flour
   plus ¼ tsp xanthan gum)
100g [1 cup] cornflour [cornstarch]
1 Tbsp vanilla bean paste
40g [3⅓ Tbsp] coconut oil, melted
3 Tbsp rum

Whisk the soy milk, sugar, white flour and cornflour together in a large bowl. Add the vanilla bean paste, melted coconut oil and rum and whisk again. Cover the bowl with plastic wrap, then place in the fridge to chill and rest for at least 24 hours. Follow steps 4–6 of the original recipe. Decorate in the same way, though instead of whipped cream, use a vegan alternative – the solids of coconut milk (after refrigerating overnight) whip up well, and you can also buy vegan cream to whip.

"You may become disenchanted sometimes, but make sure to stop and smell the roses when you do succeed."

Marshmallow Seals in a White Chocolate Igloo

For this recipe, you do need a stand mixer, as there is so much mixing involved, plus a thermometer, but other than the necessary equipment, these are quite straightforward, and will hopefully be snow mean feat! The marshmallows are flavoured with just vanilla, but you can add extracts such as rose, almond, orange or mint to flavour, if you like. The white chocolate igloo and the crème anglaise are optional, but a lot of fun to make and complete the look!

Tip: You can pipe whatever marshmallow shapes you want. You aren't limited to just seals... try polar bears, chicks (use yellow food dye in the marshmallow), cats, pigs (use pink food dye) – the possibilities are endless!

MAKES: 25–40

MARSHMALLOW SEALS
oil, for oiling
60g [⅓ cup] icing [confectioners'] sugar
60g [⅔ cup] cornflour [cornstarch]
110ml [½ cup minus 1 Tbsp] water
3 tsp powdered gelatine
170g [¾ cup plus 1½ Tbsp] caster or granulated sugar
140g [⅔ cup] liquid glucose or corn syrup
pinch of salt
1 tsp vanilla bean paste
edible black ink pen

WHITE CHOCOLATE IGLOO
400g [14oz] good-quality white chocolate, chopped into small pieces (or use vegan white chocolate)
white food dye suitable for chocolate

OR
300g [10½oz] white candy melts (this won't need tempering, but doesn't taste as good as real white chocolate)

Tip: You will have leftover melted chocolate from making the igloo, but you can save this and use it another time.

CRÈME ANGLAISE (OPTIONAL)
115ml [½ cup] double [heavy] cream (or coconut milk to make vegan)
115ml [½ cup] whole milk (or soy or other plant-based milk to make vegan)
1 tsp vanilla bean paste
4 medium egg yolks (use 1 Tbsp cornflour [cornstarch] to make vegan, plus a small pinch of ground turmeric for colour)
60g [5 Tbsp] caster or granulated sugar

1 / First, make the marshmallows. Oil 2 large baking sheets, then sift over a mixture of 40g [4½ Tbsp] of the icing sugar and 40g [¼ cup plus 1 Tbsp] of the cornflour. You want everything to be evenly and generously coated to ensure the marshmallows don't stick. Mix the remaining icing sugar and cornflour together and set aside for later.

2 / Add half the water to a stand mixer bowl, then sprinkle over the gelatine.

3 / Add the remaining water, caster sugar, liquid glucose and salt to a small saucepan, trying to avoid getting sugar stuck to the sides, and heat over a high heat, without stirring, until the mixture reaches 116°C [241°F]. At this point, put the mixer on low speed, then quickly pour the sugar syrup in. Add the vanilla bean paste, then increase the speed to high and whisk for 10–12 minutes until the mixture is thick, fluffy and pipeable.

4 / Transfer the majority of the mixture to a large piping [pastry] bag and cut a large tip. Transfer the remaining small amount to a smaller piping bag and cut a smaller tip.

5 / Use the large piping bag to pipe shapes, directly onto the oiled and powdered baking sheets, for the seal bodies – wider at the beginning and tapered smaller towards the end. You can pipe different-sized seals for variety. Next, use the smaller piping bag to add the seals' noses. Wet the end of your finger with water, then use this to push down the tip afterwards. Try to pipe as fast as you can, because the mixture will stiffen over time and become more difficult to work with. If this does happen, you can just pipe or spoon it in one even layer into another oiled and powdered tray, then you can cut it into squares later, once set.

6 / Sift the reserved icing sugar and cornflour mixture over the marshmallows and leave to completely set and dry for at least 4 hours.

7 / Meanwhile, make the white chocolate igloo. First, you will need to temper your chocolate (unless you use candy melts, in which case you can melt these in short 15-second bursts in the microwave, stirring well in between). Place a heatproof bowl (which is clean and completely dry) over a pan of boiling water, making sure the base of the bowl doesn't touch the boiling water, and add three-quarters of the finely chopped chocolate. Set the remaining one-quarter of the chocolate aside for 'seeding' the chocolate later. Stir the chocolate until it has melted and its temperature is 43°C [109°F]. Be careful not to let any water touch the chocolate, as it will seize and become unusable. Start taking the chocolate off the heat before it reaches the desired temperature, as you will find that the temperature suddenly shoots up towards the end because the bowl is very hot. Add the remaining chunks of chocolate to the bowl, stirring constantly. At this point, you can add the white food dye to colour (white chocolate is naturally yellow, so white food dye will make it whiter, which is a better colour for an igloo). Keep stirring constantly until the temperature comes down to 28–29°C [82–84°F], then pour into a clean metal or silicone half-sphere mould and place in the freezer to set for 10 minutes.

"You don't need everyone's seal of approval! You do you!"

STEP 8 ▼

STEP 10 ▼

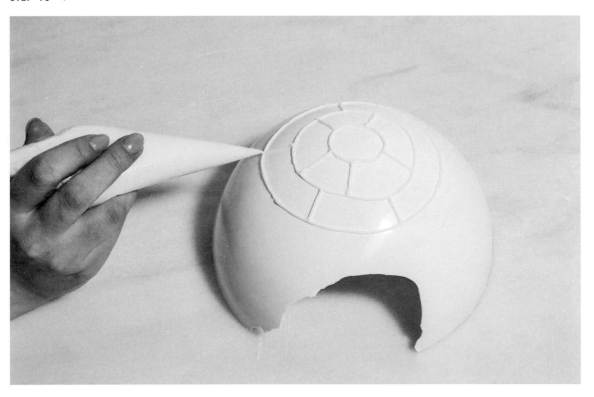

8 / Once set, the chocolate should pull away from the mould easily. Crack it on one side, working your way away from the rim, so that there is now an opening in the semi-sphere.

9 / Add the finishing details to the marshmallow seals. Use scissors to cut into the sides to create their arms, then use an edible black ink pen to add the facial details. Arrange the marshmallow seals so that they are inside the semi-sphere and peaking out through the opening.

10 / With the remaining white chocolate (you may need to re-melt it slightly so that it is pipeable again), pipe lines onto the white chocolate sphere to resemble an igloo. You can serve it like this, as it looks

impressive already, or you can do the extra step of making the crème anglaise to pour over.

Tip: If you are having difficulty piping the white chocolate onto the igloo, then use Royal Icing (page 16) instead.

TO MAKE THE CRÈME ANGLAISE
Heat the cream, milk and the vanilla bean paste in a small pan until starting to simmer. In a separate bowl, whisk the egg yolks and sugar together. Gradually whisk the hot milk mixture into the yolk mixture, making sure to add the milk gradually and to whisk constantly. Return the custard to the pan and heat until thickened enough to coat the back of a spoon.

Vegan Alternative

MARSHMALLOW SEALS

60g [⅓ cup] icing [confectioners'] sugar
60g [⅔ cup] cornflour [cornstarch]
150ml [⅔ cup] water
1½ tsp agar agar powder
150g [¾ cup] caster or granulated sugar
75g [⅓ cup] liquid glucose
pinch of salt
75ml [⅓ cup] aquafaba
⅛ tsp cream of tartar
¾ tsp xanthan gum
1 tsp vanilla bean paste

1 / Follow step 1 of the original recipe, then add half the water and the agar agar to a small pan and whisk until dissolved. Set aside for now.

2 / Mix the caster sugar, liquid glucose, salt and the remaining water together in a second small pan and heat over a high heat, without stirring, until it reaches 118°C [244°F]. Working quickly, add the aquafaba, cream of tartar and xanthan gum to a stand mixer and start whisking on high, adding the vanilla paste once it reaches soft peaks. You want to time the aquafaba reaching stiff peaks with the sugar syrup reaching temperature.

Tip: you can slow down the mixer, but don't stop it completely.

3 / When the sugar syrup is at 118°C [244°F] and the aquafaba mixture is whisked to stiff peaks, turn the mixer down to low while you pour the sugar syrup in, then increase the speed and whisk on high.

4 / Meanwhile, bring the agar agar mixture to the boil in a pan and cook for a minute or so until thickened. Add the cooked agar agar to the stand mixer and whisk on high for a further 12 minutes, or until stiff enough to pipe. Follow steps 4–10 on the original recipe (you will need to use vegan white chocolate for the igloo).

TO MAKE THE VEGAN CRÈME ANGLAISE

In a small bowl, whisk together a little of the plant-based milk (about 50g [3½ Tbsp]) with the cornflour and turmeric. Add the remaining plant milk, coconut milk, vanilla and sugar to a small pan, then add the cornflour mixture. Whisk together until combined, then heat on medium until thickened, whisking regularly to avoid lumps. Keep heating until it has thickened enough to coat the back of a spoon.

Arctic Fox Sandwich Cookies

Often when you cut out the centres for cookies, there isn't much use for them… but this recipe uses the centre cutout to create the ears and tail for these tasty-yet-adorable arctic fox cookies! The only issue is that you will probably be tempted to eat the centre cutouts, but you will have to try to resist!

MAKES: 12

ORANGE BLOSSOM GANACHE

160ml [⅔ cup] double [heavy] cream
1¼ Tbsp cornflour [cornstarch]
70g [⅓ cup plus 1 tsp] caster or granulated sugar
3½ Tbsp orange blossom water
100g [3½oz] white chocolate, chopped into small pieces

100g [7 Tbsp] butter, cubed
white food dye (optional, but this helps the ganache to look whiter in colour)

SHORTBREAD

200g [¾ cup plus 2 Tbsp] salted butter, softened at room temperature
85g [7 Tbsp] caster or granulated sugar
white food dye

220g [1⅔ cups] plain [all-purpose] flour, plus extra for dusting
50g [½ cup] cornflour [cornstarch]

PLUS

½ quantity of Royal Icing (page 16)
black food dye
icing [confectioners'] sugar, for dusting
green, red, blue and white fondant

STEP 6 ▲

1 / First, make the orange blossom ganache. Mix 30ml [2 Tbsp] of the cream with the cornflour in a small bowl. Add the remaining cream and the caster sugar to a small pan and whisk in the cornflour mixture plus 2 Tbsp of the orange blossom water. Stir over a low–medium heat until thickened. Remove from the heat and add the white chocolate, then stir until melted and smooth. Gradually add the butter (a cube at a time and stirring well after each addition), plus the remaining orange blossom water and the white food dye, if using. When smooth and everything is incorporated, transfer to a bowl, cover with plastic wrap and place in the fridge for 1–2 hours until it is firm enough to spread.

Tip: If the mixture becomes grainy or splits, gently heat it while stirring to bring it back together.

2 / Next, make the shortbread. Line 2 baking sheets that you can fit in the fridge with baking paper and set aside. Beat the butter and caster sugar together in a large bowl until smooth and fluffy. Add a little white food dye to colour, then add the flour and cornflour and mix until just combined. The dough

should be slightly sticky, but soft and easy to handle. If necessary, wrap the dough in plastic wrap and chill for 10–15 minutes until firm enough to roll out.

3 / Turn the dough out onto a well-floured surface and roll out to about 3mm [⅛in] thick. Use cutters to stamp out 24 circles, about 7.5cm [3in] in diameter, and transfer to one of the prepared baking sheets. On half the cookies, stamp out a smaller circle, about 4cm [1½in], from the lower third area (see the photos for guidance). Keep the inner-circle cutouts and place on the second baking sheet to bake as well, as they will be used for the decoration later.

4 / Chill the circles for 15 minutes in the fridge, while you preheat the oven to 160°C [325°F/Gas mark 3].

5 / Bake for 10–15 minutes until just lightly starting to colour at the edges. Leave to cool for 10 minutes on the baking sheet, then gently transfer to a wire rack to finish cooling.

6 / When the cookies are cool, cut the inner-circle shortbreads in half, then cut one-half into 2 quarters.

7 / Sandwich together the cookies using the cooled and thickened ganache. Use the two quarter pieces for the arctic fox's ears by pressing them into the ganache, and then use the half piece for its tail.

8 / Next, make the royal icing and stir in enough black food dye to achieve the desired colour, then transfer to a piping [pastry] bag and cut a small tip. Use this to pipe the face and tail details.

9 / You can also decorate the cookies with fondant holly and snowflakes in various sizes: dust a work surface with icing sugar and roll out a very small amount of green fondant. Use plunger cutters to stamp out mini pieces of holly, then repeat with blue and white fondant to make snowflakes. Use leftover icing to stick the holly pieces, plus small balls of red fondant, and the snowflakes onto the cookies to decorate.

STEP 7 ▲

STEP 8 ▲

Owl Apple Pies

Without feather ado, here are some mini apple pies, and in the cutest owl form too. You'd be wise to curl up under a blanket and enjoy these slightly warm with some cream or custard. Twit twoo.

MAKES: 12

APPLE FILLING
2 Tbsp salted butter
2½ Tbsp honey
500g [5 cups] roughly
   chopped apple
1 tsp ground cinnamon
1 tsp vanilla bean paste

PASTRY
200g [¾ cup plus 2 Tbsp]
salted butter, at room
   temperature, plus extra
   for greasing
300g [2¼ cups] plain
   [all-purpose] flour
   (to make gluten free,
   substitute with gluten-
   free flour plus ¾ tsp
   xanthan gum), plus
   extra for dusting

55g [¼ cup] caster or
   granulated sugar
1 small egg

TO DECORATE
enough flaked [slivered]
   almonds to cover
   the bottom half of
   the pies
8–10 whole pecans

3 Tbsp icing
   [confectioners'] sugar
   (optional)
24 large white chocolate
   buttons
24 dark chocolate buttons
   (or melted and piped
   dark chocolate if you
   don't have buttons)
cream or custard, to serve

1 / First, make the apple filling. Heat the butter with the honey in a frying pan until melted, then add the chopped apple. Mix to coat with butter, then add the spices and mix again. Stir intermittently over a low–medium heat until the mixture reduces down and is no longer liquid (but don't let the apples become purée – they should still be in chunks), about 10 minutes. Leave to cool while you make the pastry.

2 / To make the pastry, grease a 12-hole muffin tray with butter. Add the flour (or gluten-free flour plus xanthan gum) to a large bowl. Chop the butter and add it to the bowl, then rub it into the flour until it resembles fine breadcrumbs. Don't overwork. Stir in the caster sugar. Beat the egg in a separate small bowl, then add 2 Tbsp to the main mixing bowl and stir, gradually combining it with the rest of the mixture. When the egg is stirred through, use your hands to form the pastry into a ball.

3 / Roll out the pastry on a well floured surface as thinly as you can, then use a round cutter to stamp out 12 circles. Use your fingers to gently guide each circle of pastry into each muffin hole. Prick the bases with a fork 2–3 times, then refrigerate for 20 minutes. Preheat the oven to 180°C [350°F/Gas mark 4].

4 / Spoon the apple filling into each pastry hole. Use a little water to wet the rim of the pastry shells, then stamp out 12 smaller circles of pastry and use as a lid for each tart. Press down with your fingers to ensure the pastry adheres. Brush with beaten egg (you can use the leftover from making the pastry), then arrange flaked almonds on the bottom half. Chop a pecan into a thinner piece and use this for the owl's nose in the centre of the pie. You will add the eyes and eyebrows after baking, so for now, cut 2 slits in the pastry where the eyes will be (this will also help moisture escape from the pie while baking).

5 / Bake for 20 minutes, or until golden brown. Leave to cool in the tin for 10–15 minutes, then slide out and place on a wire rack to finish cooling.

6 / When cool, finish decorating the pies. You can make edible glue by placing the icing sugar in a small bowl and stirring in a tiny amount of water, a drop at a time, to make a paste, or using some melted chocolate. Use this to stick on white and dark chocolate buttons for the eyes and thin slices of pecans for the eyebrows. Serve with some cream or custard for extra deliciousness.

INDEX

- INDEX -

Acknowledgements

I'm so grateful to everyone around me who has directly and indirectly made this book happen!

My first thank you is of course to Nabil, my partner and best friend. I love that through supporting me, you've become a pretty good baker yourself now as well as my Number One food taster! PLUS our kittens (fast becoming grown cats!), Inki and Mochi. Thanks for trying to eat any cream or butter I leave unattended for just a second! And trying to steal my attention away whenever I try to bake anything that isn't cat themed.

Thank you to my mum, Kenneth, Kevan, Julian, Crystal, Callum, Aiden and Jonny, Lydia, and Omer. Also my Auntie Audrey, Auntie Sandra, Uncle Yan Teo. Plus the rest of my family around the world.

To the whole team at Quadrille – you have all been incredible once again. Special mentions to Céline Hughes for being a total star and believing in me. Plus Alicia House for the beautiful book design! And to Ellis Parrinder for being a brilliant support and taking incredible photos to make my bakes shine, as always! And to Sarah Hardy for being the best kitchen buddy EVER! And Charlie Phillips for the fab props. You have all been a joy to work with (though it didn't feel like work!) and the best team members.

And thank you to Vivienne Clore for helping me to get a SECOND book out! Didn't think the first would happen, let alone the second!

To my most fabulous friends EJ and JJ (and Hercules!), Siân, Charlotte and Simon (and Sinda and Otis of course!). I don't know where I'd be without you all! EJ and JJ – thanks for the jokes! Sian – thank you for the Welsh baking advice. Simon and Charlotte – thank you for occasionally taking me out of baking world by playing Mario Kart with me (I am still the champion mwahaha).

And I am indebted to everyone at Love Productions who gave me the opportunity to be on the *Bake Off* and opened up my world. And thank you to all my *Bake Off* family and friends I've met through baking.

I am also grateful to Linda van den Berg (your illustrations always delight!), Danni Hooker (for my lovely hair and make-up yet again!), Mary Kate McDevitt (always delivering the most beautiful title lettering!), and the crew at Travelling Man.

Also thanks to Aaron Copping, Abigail Jill Harding, Alex Few, Alicia Hazzard, Amy Bellwood, Anna Appleby, Biserka Stringer-Horne, Chip and Kim, Chloe Green, Dan Corbridge, Diane and Len Marlow, Esther and James, Gemma Hartshorn, Gerry Taylor, Holly Homsi, Ian Salmon, Ivan Salazar, James and Helen, Jimmy Aquino, Jules Raffensperger, Lisa, Darren and Iona, Luke Cridland, Maeve Bargman, Martha Limburg, Martha and Gloria, Mark, Jenny, Lottie and Grayson, Matt and Frank, Matt Taylor, Rachel Dawson, Renée Senogles, Rick Meeson, Richard Starkings, Sam Butt, Sarah and Alan, Sarah and Chris, Steve Emmott, Tracy and Dan, and all the James family: Pippa, Sammie, Millie, Paul and Andrea.

And to everyone who has ever said something kind or positive to me, or taught me something new – thank you.

I am beyond grateful to all of you who have made this book a reality.

PUBLISHING DIRECTOR: Sarah Lavelle
SENIOR COMMISSIONING EDITOR: Céline Hughes
DESIGNER: Alicia House
PHOTOGRAPHER: Ellis Parrinder
ASSISTANT FOOD STYLIST: Sarah Hardy
PROP STYLIST: Charlie Phillips
HAIR & MAKE-UP: Danni Hooker
HEAD OF PRODUCTION: Stephen Lang
PRODUCTION CONTROLLER: Katie Jarvis

Published in 2020 by Quadrille,
an imprint of Hardie Grant Publishing

QUADRILLE
52–54 Southwark Street
London SE1 1UN
quadrille.com

All rights reserved. No part of this publication may be
reproduced, stored in a retrieval system or transmitted
in any form by any means, electronic, mechanical,
photocopying, recording or otherwise, without the
prior written permission of the publishers and copyright
holders. The moral rights of the author have been
asserted.

Cataloguing in Publication Data: a catalogue record for
this book is available from the British Library.

Text © Kim-Joy 2020
Photography © Ellis Parrinder 2020
Design and layouts © Quadrille 2020

ISBN 978 1 78713 582 6

Printed in China

Reprinted in 2020
10 9 8 7 6 5 4 3 2